TERRORIST PSYCHOTIC: MARY PATTON

TERRORIST PSYCHOTIC: MARY PATTON

Martin Mongiello

The American Revolutionary War Living History Center
2019

Copyright © 2019 by Martin CJ Mongiello

All rights reserved. This book or any portion thereof may not be reproduced or used in any manner whatsoever without the express written permission of the publisher except for the use of brief quotations in a book review or scholarly journal.

First Printing: 2019

ISBN 978-0-359-36465-7

The American Revolutionary War Living History Center
301 Cleveland Avenue
Grover, NC 28073

www.arwlhc.com

Ordering Information:

Special discounts are available on quantity purchases by corporations, associations, educators, and others. For details, contact the publisher at the above-listed address.

U.S. trade bookstores and wholesalers: Please contact The American Revolutionary War Living History Center. Tel: (704) 490-3947.

Dedication

This book is dedicated to the continuing efforts of the Charlotte Museum of History, NC, the Kings Mountain History Museum, NC, and Sycamore Shoals State Park, TN, **the many sponsors who keep them financially alive**, *and the citizens and families of the region. May they remain forever grateful for the historic win at the battle of King's Mountain, which scared General Cornwallis into evacuating Charlotte.*

The tactical advantages provided from over the mountains by one professional businesswoman and expert black powder maker shall forever be remembered. She was coy, smart, diligent, and giving.

Mary Patton shattered glass ceilings for a woman in the 1700s and let many a man know it was #TimesUp! before he even had a chance to act up.

With your purchase, you are helping to keep history alive and to share the enormous role that women have had throughout time and history.

For my wife Stormy, my son James Thomas, and my daughter Rania.

Contents

Acknowledgments vii

Introduction 1

Chapter 1: We piss on Major Ferguson's British and lifeless body 3

Chapter 2: When men rudely interrupt women in meetings 11

Chapter 3: Officer's swords are good for stabbing prisoner's to death 17

Chapter 4: The daily work of a "deviant and rebel," Mary Patton 23

Chapter 5: Winning the war and becoming a wealthy landowner 30

Chapter 6: The family today, a family of love 38

Chapter 7: My grandchildren do not have the same accent as I 42

Index 51

Bibliography 57

Acknowledgments

I want to thank the many museum historians and teachers that have helped me along the way. We must honor our teachers, museum professionals, and professors correctly.

Consider that close to 86% of prisoners in the most extensive prison system on earth (America) are functionally illiterate. Moreover, that 900,000 of those are black Americans (40% of all prisoners), yet they are only 12%[1] of the US population. If more education made it through to the 2.2 million total in prison, we would do better. Given the most recent strikes by teachers, I want to thank them and encourage you the reader to support fair pay for them.

I am very appreciative of my Professors and Doctors at The City Colleges of Chicago, Troy State University, Almeda College and University, The Art Institute of Charlotte, The Art Institute of Pittsburgh, and Lenoir Rhyne University. However, especially Travis McVey, Antwain Thomas, Orlando Herrera, Doctor Craig Schreiber, Adria Focht, Scott Syfert, Mark Anthony, David Sherrill (as Doctor Franklin), Howard Burnham, Ken Unnasch, David Unnasch, Kim Hambright, Pastor Deneise Deter Liss, Edith Morgan, Emmy nominated producer Carl White, NC Speaker of the House Tim Moore, **Rick Moore**, my mom and dad, Jason Falls, Pastor Will Upchurch, Frank Panzone, Lance Bacchia, Luciano Bacchia, Pastor Reg Alexander, Pastor Richard Smith, Mayor Bill Willis, William Richard King, Carole Plonk Haas Gravagno, Doctor Hank Weddington, Doctor Leslie McKesson, Doctor Lisa Fournier, Doctor Dean, and Anne Ornish, Doctor David Jones, Doctor Thomas Toglia, Doctor Thomas Turner, and Professor Laura Hope-Gill. Some of my greatest teachers have been my former Headmaster and Director of Education, Allan B. Miller, of Palm Beach, Florida, Captain Patrick J. Casey, (Ret.), USN, Vice Admiral Albert Konetzni, Jr., (Ret.) (Big Al the Sailor's pal), USN, Admiral (four-star) Cecil D. Haney, (Ret.), USN, Rear Admiral Marc Pelaez, (Ret.), USN, and Rear Admiral Joseph J. Krol, Jr., (Ret.), USN

I am truly blessed to have had them help me to grow and I am forever grateful.

---

[1] Tripp, B. (2018). Incarcerated African American fathers: Exploring changes in family relationships and the father identity. In Impacts of incarceration on the African American family (pp. 17-32): Routledge.

Dear Ludy,

Thank you so much for all of your plays & support of The Lincoln Legend!! :)

[signature] 2-9-20

Introduction

This IS NOT a children's book to be left around where they can read it. This book is not titled nor written to provide what you are looking for or want. It's written in the truth of what many do not like, seek to hide, and bury in the secrecy of lies, or just doesn't fit the typical National Park Service, "APPROVED FOR SALE" list. It's written in the style of creative non-fiction which was a requirement of the Master's degree class I was taking in the Thomas Wolfe Institute.

If the English word of Terrorist had existed in the eighteenth century, the British would have used it regarding bomb makers, bullet pourers, and the rebels meeting in basements to make such. They spoke of those illegally making black powder in mass quantities of being outlaws, psychos, deviants, variants, and stealing the King's excrement which <u>by law was owned by the crown</u> in every outhouse.

This book may be considered to contain the vulgarity of war or the filth of indignity towards American or British people. Depending on your views, it could incite anger or rage within you. I have many, many English friends. Whichever they prefer, I am respectful and oblige them in honor of our modern relationship of care, sharing, and kindness between our two countries. Many of them worship in the Anglican faith, and I love them. No one was more excited and overjoyed than my wife and I to watch Princess Meghan get married to Prince Harry! In 2018 it was a beautiful event for American-UK relations as well as blacks and whites. The manner within which Queen Elizabeth conducted herself was remarkable.

Long before the #MeToo and TimesUp! movements I wrote about, published articles and advocated for women. I served in the military and presently hold a 30-year retired certificate of service. I lived inside of the ocean on six submarines and cared for about 36 total subs. I don't know how many I have actually been on at sea but do have over eight years of entire sea time and six years of overseas service on top of that. I lived on three continents and was stationed in Asia, Hawaii, and Europe working with women in different wars. I wanted to retire at sea, on a Sacramento-class fast combat support ship while most other senior sailors do their last tour at a shore base. I also wanted to get my Surface Warfare pin (a military warfare device worn on uniforms after qualifying through practical exams and learning) to add to my Submarine Warfare pin. To do that, I served onboard a massive ship of 796 feet long, 107 feet wide, drawing 38 feet down into the water at 57,000 tons with 636 sailors onboard. I had previously been on a half-dozen other large ships so enjoyed them.

[**The guided-missile cruiser USS Anzio (CG 68), Nimitz-class aircraft carrier USS Dwight D. Eisenhower (CVN 69), and amphibious assault ship USS Saipan (LHA 2) sail in formation.** Photo by Mass Communication Specialist Seaman Patrick W. Mullen III.]

Half of our crew were ladies, and I always treated them with the awe of respect and watching Wonder Woman at work. Women in War are fascinating and motivated human beings today contributing to the effort in physical, dangerous, life-threatening work. It often involved weapons, bombs, and operating engine rooms in Operation Iraqi Freedom. I worked with female pilots and Commanding Officers of carriers, like Captain Norma Lee Hackney of the USS Saipan (LHA-2) with 1500 Marines onboard her ship and 1000 crew. I watched Gunners Mate Kerri (Tuttle) Johann fire all types of weapons and drive bomb racks in the pouring rain of a pitching deck at sea. My wife, Stormy, worked in the military on Navy jet and helicopter engines as a mechanic extraordinaire. Moreover, when I was injured they flew me back to Norma Lee's carrier to be operated on during Operation Enduring Freedom (Afghanistan), I knew I was in good hands.

Women have been involved in war, like Mary Patton, for a long time – often doing the gritty and hard work of dangerously making black powder. As you'll see, Mary becomes known as one of our area sheroes for producing premium weapons grade products. I call her Batwoman because she has a sharp tongue and the gumption to mark and keep secret bat cave maps where she obtains her poop to make nitrate. But you'll read about that soon enough.

Chapter 1: We piss on Major Ferguson's British and lifeless body

"Once ah saw the bastud, Major Ferguson, in mee sights, dead foaking on, ah pulled mee hair trigger on Scot-Irish Red an uh shot him through his mined!" boasted McKee. "Been shootin with that feefty cal(iber) rifle named Scot-Irish Red since ah was a wee baby an ah coult shoot a squirrel from a leemb - 300 foot away if'n ah wanted it."

These were not people to antagonize, apparently, for each one was a marksman and sharpshooter with little or nothing to live for other than the treasured warrior cult-like clan family pride.[2] Which was a thing to protect or take a sharpened dirk and press your own neck down hard on it? No one is giving up their pride or reputation let alone family honor. Especially in Appalachia parts[3] and all throughout the backcountry, upcountry, and Kentucky.[4] You could call him on it, any one of them, in fact, "oh really, let me see you shoot a squirrel right now, bitch, off of a limb?" But you would just lose that bet.

James McKee had lost his half-brother in the battle of King's Mountain, Major William Chronicle, and was in a sullen mood, yet happy that they had won. Now marching the 800+ prisoners around the countryside was wearing on his and everyone's nerves. Emasculating the British officers in their red coats and gold braid on their shoulders was a bit of fun to be had or at least until they tried to attack you. Why then we get to shoot you, or better yet, another opportunity for a good knife fight to the death.

"But Colonel Sevier, if you could please just have these backwater men stop threatening my men," stated the British Surgeon Dr. Uzal Johnson, now a prisoner himself. "As a Doctor,

---

[2] The cultural identity of outdoorsman warriors is legendary in the Scottish and Irish lifestyle. Webb, J. H. (2005). Born fighting: how the Scots-Irish shaped America: Random House Digital, Inc.

[3] Hirschman, E., Brown, S., & Maclaran, P. (2007). Two Continents, One Culture: The Scotch-Irish in Southern Appalachia: The Overmountain Press.

[4] In these parts, we have about 250,000 people living somewhat rugged in the year of 1780 in parts we call the backcountry, mean-ing West, and up-country being a name used for upstate South Carolina. Kentucky is not a state yet but can be a rather broad term meaning anything uncivilized in the West. And by West, I mean not far past Dollywood and Gatlinburg. Indeed, there is "the West." But, it's not like John Wayne in a Western film yet, blowing men away with six-guns. Be mindful when you see the word, "Kentucky," written in family letters and doing genealogical research.

I realize we are all exhausted, and there is little to eat. Each man on both sides is starving. Telling others, John, how urinating all over our commander's face was funny is not helping the blimey situation. Threatening to kill us, hang us, and more is not humane in the code of conduct. John, Colonel John Sevier of North Carolina spoke victoriously and authoritatively, "I will talk with them again about it, but we are most likely going to conduct some sort of court-martial at one of the larger homes nearby, Uzal. A number of your men have been identified as criminals, and I can't say it's going to be pretty. And I can't hide a criminal who has killed, stolen, raped, or burned victims in these parts. I realize that you are very educated and from New Jersey with stagecoaches, taverns, and colleges, but you have to realize." "Excuse me," Dr. Johnson interrupted, "but realize what, a man showing others his penis and flopping it up and down last night as he laughed out loud with others drinking whiskey on an empty stomach? And boasting about how he pissed into the open mouth of a dead British officer with other men undoing their pants for the same?"

Sevier knew what had happened and had ordered an end to that behavior in the chaos and cries for water after the battle had ended. "I had been one of the first to order those men to stop that and mind you it was a very few only who did that, not our entire army, so don't try to characterize us as barbarians as a whole. And don't you make reports to that effect as I will dispute it in writing, sir." Colonel Sevier would later become the statesman Governor of two states in America but knew well the ferocity of the clansmen warrior getting their revenge for the battle losses in Scotland at Culloden[5] and destroying the British armies once and for all. Murtagh Fraser had said it best to him in Wilmington one day, "a new world so a new ending this time around."

His response shocked the Surgeon, "I can only offer you Stinking Billy flowers today, Doctor." He was referring to the same flower that the British call Sweet William in honor of the Duke of Cumberland, Prince William, erasing Scotland from the maps and taking it at the battle of Culloden for the United Kingdom.

---

[5] Pollard, T. (2009). Culloden: the history and archaeology of the last clan battle: Pen and Sword Military.

Later that night, Johnson listened to more taunting about the upcoming hangings to be after the fires had near burned down, directed at British supporter Colonel Ambrose Mills, by a Hessian deserter who had signed up with the rebels named Gunther. "And for killing our family," several men were pelting him, "that's right you shate," you'll be one of the first we watch kick out with a snapped neck you dirty little man. You're the one who turned in Captain Benjamin (they were yelling about Captain Benjamin Merrill) to Governor Tryon. And that butcher had him slightly hung until he almost died, got him down, cut open his stomach with a blade, removed all of the intestines for being drawn and quartered and then attached both arms and legs to four separate horses to be ripped apart. And you call that responsible government? You call that humane treatment of prisoners and what is written in the law for punishments? Do you wonder why we are so fucking stirred up around here in Western North Carolina? When you goddamned butchers took his fucking head and placed it onto a pole right outside of Tryon Palace? You do realize that people 100 years from now, in 1880, or the year of 1980, or 2080 are going to read about what you did, and know it!?"

It was getting worse; he began thinking privately.

The surgeon realized that the Governor Tryon of New York he had met and dined with should never have been promoted by his Majesty, George the III. If they had known the things, he did down here in NC as the Governor.

If he had only known the things he did to the Regulators down here, he would have never signed up for this expedition with Major Patrick Ferguson. Getting out here with the locals was now getting worse and finding out these supposed truths was becoming weirder as so many of them were animated and angry.

The sweet potato dinner had not been much to eat, and the starving rebels evidently had not eaten in two days. Conversely, the day of the battle, Saturday, steaks had been served to all of the British forces at King's Mountain with potatoes prepared of 1400 portions to have some extra in case Dragoons showed up.

The attack went on, bitterly as darkness was setting in earlier this time of year.

"You send the Sheriff around here to intimidate and threaten us, and then he shows back up the next day to do tax collection. Did you not learn anything from the 13th and 14th-century stories of, of, of bastards like this? Of the Sheriff of Nottingham and Robin Hood. And then, AND THEN, the rip-off artist takes half of the taxes for his own pocket!"

A quick swig from his flask again, again, and again, some of which dripped down his glistening lips and face. It electrified his veins and animated his open hand to clench up into the shape of a balled fist where parts of the fingers turned white from squeezed blood, up and down the manacle and you could see he hurt himself by doing it and eased up his clinch.

"And the other half gets turned in to build a fancy castle for Governor Tryon? Is that what you think we need more of in America, another fucking castle!? And families go there now to vacation and adore that palace, do they?" Why I wouldn't take a raw shit on the pathway of that beautiful place let alone stop to spit on the walkway." He turned directly away from the prisoner, crushing a twig under his hand-tooled leather shoes as if to walk away, but then swung and backed his ass down to Mill's face releasing a long, sickening fart through his linen, used-to-be-white pants with the dirty knees - that obviously was a slightly wet release. "Somebody needs to go wipe," came out of the crowd of men laughing but couldn't be determined as to who said it. And no one was helping to point to who said it.

The cold air of Fall luckily diminished part of the fecal gas as the trees lost a few more leaves in a thankful breeze. Still, though, Mills threw himself down on the ground to further avoid it, by leaning to his left, despite his hands tied behind his back. It was enough to make your hair fall out of the scalp or burn the face as poison or flame would.

"Now that got some beef gravy with it!" someone else snickered out and spat over towards Mills with a big-throated hack and lungy pull of flem. It didn't take long for others to begin spitting also and pulling up hacks to fire over. A few had colds, and you could hear a week-long cough in some by the stringiness of the mucus that just sounded green or yellow. Now constant spitting and hacking took its time, and Gunther took a break as it seemed minutes or ten minutes of hawking spit over at the red-coated back continued. "Fucking jerk," "bastard and bitch," "here's for you whore," "pussy," "satanicus," "die now lobster," and many other greetings were added in out of frustration as horses nickered in the night possibly scared as well, or alerted to the growing mob-like slanders and protectively stamped their feet into no dust, strong grassy bladed fields.

"It's nothing exceptional to look at, your shitty Tryon Palace unless you want to admire the medicines our families cannot afford, the grandparents that have died in its wake and everything ever named Tryon. Did they ever find the North Carolina men who burned Governor Tryon's house down to the ground at 2:30 in the morning in New York after he had been promoted to that colony!? No, they didn't, what a pity that happened as we followed him all the way up there."

The stars in a clear sky listened shamefully at the truth and looked down on ragged faces that were witnessed as dirty and unclean shaven. It takes Orion until around nine-ish at night to come across the Eastern side of this part of the earth this time of year, and someone began to point and nod their head to distinguish the belt, sword, and shield. Still, though, most were immersed at what was in point of fact happening and being said. They either didn't know the truth, couldn't read the newspapers, or got tired of waiting two weeks to find one in a market, or home, or even being resold for the fifth time as, "precious."

"People who know the truth know why we want to kill people like you," Gunther went on. "You just hung 40 some patriots in Camden, at Augusta, and in Ninety-Six. And what was their crime? Why I'll tell you what it was, each town was informed they were merely on the wrong side so were being hung. Colonel Shelby knows this truth, and so does Colonel Hampton. They didn't commit any war crimes, and they weren't spies or anything. So now we'll hang a few of you in retaliation for your sickening killings. And everything to do with you and Tryon Street, Tryon Mountain, Tryon County, Tryon School, Tryon Park, and Tryon Palace[6] need to be exterminated and removed from the face of the earth!" He was down in his face now with drool coming out of his mouth as he cursed and menaced with his arms. He

---

[6] Today tax dollars continue to flood into Tryon Palace by the tens of millions as it is celebrated as a critical tourism spot amongst unknowing Patriots. Similarly, many streets and places in New York and North Carolina continue to be enjoyed and cherished due to the name of Governor Tryon by those who don't know how many of their family he had hunted and killed.

punched Colonel Mills in the mouth as the others jeered him on. "Do you like that, when a private punches a Colonel in his ugly whore of a face!?"

At this point, Colonel Hampton **(featured in the first ever commissioned painting completed in US history – all rights owned by author)** arrived and barked down the ruckus. He knew things were getting out of control and hundreds starving were getting meaner by the minute and swigging corn whiskey on empty stomachs might not be helping.

"I may be in my seventies, but we've got some big days ahead of us what with the court martials, hangings, and marching all over our state. Now you men stop this consternation and noise and get to laying down. As an Englishman myself born and raised there – no one is angrier over the way we have been treated here. I assure yee all[7] that we will be getting to the bottom of all of this. We won the battle so be proud and stop abusing them."

Colonel Cleaveland **(featured in the first ever commissioned painting completed in US history – all rights owned by author)** came over also and physically picked Gunther up by the fronting of his jacket, lifting him a few inches up off the ground, and told him, "Don't make me throw you down drunk into bed tonight boy. Colonel Hambright was almost killed in action, and he would be ashamed of you hitting an asshole."

---

[7] "Yee all," was a very common British saying and later became the word Y'all. All Y'alls became the plural version of Y'all and You All is used today to address a group of people gathered together.

At which point several men got his theme and laughed about him calling Colonel Mills and asshole, but themselves didn't want any part of the massive, 300 pound Benjamin Cleaveland. Or was it 400 pounds? Whatever it was, it would kick your ass. Gunther had one parting comment, "Gilkey, McFall, Bibby, Hobbs, and you Mills, you and many others - you swing soon."

'GOODNIGHT GUNTHER, THANK YOU FOR ONE MORE COMMENT, GOODNIGHT GUNTHER, GOOD NIGHT EACH OF YOU," Cleaveland snapped with his mitts on his adamant sides of his waistcoat glaring at them in the dark. You couldn't really see him glaring, It was pretty dark, but you could hear him glaring. He mentioned to Hampton, "Do you think anyone realizes that a woman's skill and work helped tactically to beat the most powerful army on earth - backed by the richest war chest in history?"

Hampton sneered, "If they only knew our women! Someday I'd like to unleash them into our forces just to watch an ass-whipping of men like these British see their power."

"It's sure to lead to their defeat this time and shrink up the empire, " Cleaveland speculated. "It's forbidden for girls to learn most anything there, to do real work, own companies, become a success – and just look at how successful this campaign has been in winning the battles we have won," he deduced.

Hampton was walking away tired and obviously off to find some sleep himself, somewhere, who knows where, over there, his back to Benjamin and not turning the slightest to bark, "I'm sure we blokes will get and take all of the credit though, we always do."

And why not - were the private thoughts of many close enough to have heard what they may have said. Is that what they said? After all, as men, we take whatever we want, we write the history books, we run the governments, we ram our fucking cocks into pussies whenever we want, and we write the laws. We command the earth, killing, war, taxes, history and we take. Anything. Anywhere. Anytime.

Bitch.

Chapter 2: When men rudely interrupt women in meetings

For so long the difference between life and death to tame the insect-filled wilderness with snakes and wild beasts that would eat children, a man, a woman – alive, had been her battle. These trips of 1770 through the early 1800s bumped along in the Pennsylvania made schooner wagon even knocking Mary out on three occasions of thirty-years time onto the ground. She always had vowed to keep that record limited to two times, maximum.

Alas.

Falling asleep on the bench sitting upright sucked, unless you were leaning against a loved one.

Hole in the road.

Now that will wake you up!

Axles snapped?

Too many times.

Stuck in a deeper than we thought hole but was damnation covered up with murky water so we couldn't see how deep a hole it was - hole.

Wheel pins lost in the bushes. Spokes cracked. Such was the life and lore of backroad travels. After all, this wasn't the turnpike from Philadelphia to Lancaster! Her husband John had caught her, or grabbed her arm, at least a dozen more times and saved her as many times she had him from falling out and hitting the road or a tree.

They traveled through Charlottetown (Charlottesburg, Charlotte) all the way to Wilmington often and down to Savannah and Charlestown (Charleston). At times she sold alone and on horseback, even. They most often used Walker's ferry to cross the Catawba River.

And then it happened. "Why we tie ourselves in with some line[8] every time!" he near bellowed in his sailor's outfit. "It ain't no different than learning that trick at sea when up on deck in a storm, and these here prairie schooners[9] pitch and buck, back and fro like Poseidon's trident is stabbin' away at your boat."

Shankless Buckeye was quite a character to meet in Captain James Jack's Tavern while staying the night over with John in Charlottetown. Most likely a liar and storyteller with a virtuous notion. But it was a good idea, seeing how he had noticed John had a black eye. But what kind of a name is, Shankless? Mary was sure it was his nickname and not a real name.

"Well it's on my dang birth certificate!" he provided to her hubby and rocked his pewter tankard down on the shaky table slopping some minor foam out and onto the used to be dry wood. "Now don't tell Sam Adams I spilled some o' his beer, but, well, it is now, I'll bring the paper next time straight away to your inspection if ya want?" he offered. Oh God, John (she thought) don't get him so animated. Not again this time.

"Now, Shackled (she kidded) I'll be expecting to examine your birth papers with ma magnifying glass!" Forget it, let's animate him tonight. Why not!?

"Oh, I will fer sure, and let me tell you a thing or two," he interrupted.

So she boldly interrupted him, "Now don't interrupt me while I'm interrupting you, Shankup. Shackled when next we meet, why I'll have the County Magistrate, Hez Alexander[10] look over these supposed documents" Mary forcefully instigated.

"My name is Shankless."

---

[8] In the Navy rope is called line and sailors and soldiers can be particularly funny about which word is right.

[9] A slang term for sailing the prairie, or amber waves of grain that look like billowing oceans in your wagon across vast stretches of open land. The best wagons built come from a Pennsylvania valley named Conestoga. You may have heard about the Conestoga wagon. Families are taught how to also use them to ford rivers as they actually are also a boat

[10] Hez is a shorted version for Hezekiah Alexander that he used himself in signing documents and receipts. A noted and excellent public speaker he was appointed county magistrate by the hated and vicious British Governor William Tryon in 1768. He served as county magistrate until 1794. He turned sides after repeatedly warning Governor Tryon about taxing people and using the money only for the Anglican church, restrictions on Presbyterian ministers, King George's rejection of the Queen's College charter and many, many other insulting and derogatory actions.

"Of course it is," Mary replied.

She wanted to fire him up near that rough stone fireplace he was warming himself at and leaning over their table. He was so much fun to laugh with, she guessed, despite his awful red beard twisted in uncombed ways and allowed to grow free, like a shrub, like a wild bush. Was that food in the shrub he didn't even notice? Or a small bird nesting...

They would only see him and his knee stockings once or twice a year. It was always worth it. Why you could notice him a half mile away by the damned beard alone!

It seemed like his gape-mouthed jaw needed to drool down on his own pant-leg as he couldn't believe she had interrupted him. A human male. A man. But she did. And he realized that his own thoughts of raping her on the floor immediately, stabbing, shooting, killing John, rallying the men to kill and rape her in the bar, all of those fleeting ideas that raced through his mind, sudden coping mechanisms to shut her fucking mouth for good, well, it just seemed better to have her as an ally than a dead enemy, or a living enemy. She was obviously the type of woman that kept a hidden knife in her ass cheeks, or on a leg holster, or in the boot and would cut your goddam ball sack the fuck off during a raping. She was the type of whore (that's what he called her in his mind due to being interrupted) that would have two or three knives hidden around ankles, breast, and ass. Fucking cunt and slut, why are you even in here with men talking? He raged secretly inside wondering what to do. There's nothing more goddamned worse than a titty whore in business, whores that use their throat to speak out loud, whores teaching in colleges, whores with degrees and whores with professions that had to be dealt with. And he knew how to deal with cavewomen all bent over for his pleasure one after the other. Since all women are whores the best thing for them is fucking. Or a beating in a man's world.

Mary paid for his drink to buy his allegiance and assure their safety.

Such was the character of many men only supported by meek women who allowed and encouraged the world to operate as it did, for so long. That's how she felt.

And let's not forget when returning home from these long trips, the strongbox was always carried in by two stout men and filled with gold, jewels, silver, Spanish and Portuguese coins[11], silver and gold Pound Scots coins, Irish Pound coin, assorted states paper money, shillings, crowns, guinea, and pound sterling backed by gold. Sir Isaac Newton, Master of the Royal Mint, had switched it from being supported by silver in 1717.[12] Mary was growing quite rich and purchasing thousands of acres of land very slowly and diligently. She sold her powder for a dollar a pound on these trips. She and John would often bring a guard with them to watch the new wagon they had made in the Conestoga Valley of Pennsylvania where they formerly lived nearby in Carlisle.

This time it was Seamus (a strong Irish immigrant like John) who slept outside to watch the hidden money and powder. He had been a guest on the Hezekiah Alexander lands by Charlottetown before moving further West and told them stories of the secret signals in the upstairs windows. Many men left home during the British occupation of that town, for their own safety, and Mother's (like Mary Sample Alexander) hung clandestine indicators to let sons know they could come back home to resupply quickly – and the evacuate out again. He was a very trusted protector.

So why was he at the table now, which gave Shankless new caution to be reminded they had another man with them who was very strong. And he eyed him up and down assessing attacking him, possibly later, or another time, or tonight, next time, now, no, not now. Something men do a lot of (can I take this guy) every time they meet someone.

---

[11] In reality, hidden and obsolete coins were carried over from Europe and revealed themselves across the colonies along with new paper money printed during the war. Mary accepted and understood the values of dozens of different countries coins and kept a record of it in her mind and books. Not everyone would accept old world coinage.

[12] You may recall American currency was at one time supported by gold, and then eventually silver. Which is stronger? Today it is just cotton rag and backed by nothing. In 2019, according to the Federal Reserve, there is about $1.72 trillion in circulation. America harvests about $560 million in new notes per year. British counterfeiting during the war was so real it almost brought the colonies to its knees. Their engravers and replicators flooded our world, and this is an effective wartime stratagem employed by many countries. Combat is not always the only way to kill people.

Which is why she and John always had a room with the window cracked next to the wagon allowed to be pulled close to the building just for them. A coin for the owner ever got that approved.

"Sally New River[13] is outside on her business with some men and asked if you remembered her, and she wants powder." "Of course," Mary replied, I remember her well and recently heard more about her grandfather King Hagler."[14]

She added, "women in this tribe own their own companies, they are different. But she won't come in here, Seamus. Let me go outside."

"What, a squaw[15] that owns a company!?" outlandishly he waived his ginger-haired arms as the swaying red beard tracked. "Why not bring her in since this is a women's business meeting!?" Shankless roared. "Or the King can come in also. Hell, let's meet a King!"

"He's dead for some time now, and this group of Indians has learned about the liquor not being good for them. This is a business matter so stay in here and don't bother us."

As Mary stood up, she revealed under her blue woolen cloak, and tapped, two long brown wood 1739 Dragoons[16] on a thick, worn black belt to warn him and sternly offered, "These Catawba warrior women also carry pistols and do business with many. They're not like other tribal women. If the bald earring wearing Captain Redhead is with her, you won't want to agitate him either. Give us a minute, and I'll buy your next quart."

---

[13] Sally New River is an extremely famous land-owner and warrior shero of the Catawba American Indian Nation. They controlled and owned most all of what is now called the state of South Carolina and large amounts of land in what is now called North Carolina. Today their reservation and Long House headquarters is located in Rock Hill, SC.

[14] King Hagler is also an extremely famous Chief or King of the Catawba American Indian Nation. He lived from 1749 to 1763 and was a powerful ally as the Catawba are known into today for being excellent warfighters. Many white elements and factions courted the Catawba warriors for that reason and King Hagler was an excellent diplomat and military leader in battle and war.

[15] Considered a disgusting and filthy word today for anyone to use. Especially since the Catawba do not consider man or woman superior to one another in their rules of society. It is a cultural shock to see whites practice it.

[16] These are rather larger hand-held pistols, or small cannons, typically used on horseback by Dragoons.

Well, that was all he needed to hear as she motioned in the air to the girl to mark a Q on the blackboard behind the bar for her account and pointed to his back motioning with one finger up. She would pay for her P's and Q's in the morning with black dust just like she paid for all of her lodgings. It was better than having gold at times. It could win wars and tip scales.

And HE was with her. This was, after all, the Indian nation which formerly owned most of Carolina long before the North and South Carolina had been created that had sided with the colonists to build America. The Cherokee had decided to go with the British and stop any formation of the United Colonies, or the United States. Captain Redhead **(featured in the first ever commissioned painting completed in US history by Jeff Trexler – all rights owned by author)** had helped scout for many American victories and was a well-known warrior. "Tanakɛ," John greeted (Hello). "Wiitcaware tineyedo?" said Mary (How are you? A version used at night).

Chapter 3: Officer's swords are good for stabbing prisoner's to death

Another night of starving had passed for the thousands assembled, another day of marching, included in this were hundreds of British prisoners from the recent battle of King's Mountain being guarded by the victors. The mob was still on its way West for upcoming trials to be held at Biggerstaff's Plantation, a bit South of what would soon be settled as Morristown[17] and later called the Asheville.[18] Where Hernando de Soto had come through on his expeditions of 1540.[19] Around 3 am a crash half-scared the hell out of several hundred when too many birds gathered on an oak tree and shattered a multi-hundred-pound limb off of it.

Ishmael recalled how he had only heard about the works of the famed Englishman John Lawson as a kid but knew himself they were actually correct. Yes, flocks of a million birds flew around, John Lawson had not written lies in his book about America in the early 1700s. Yet newcomers always asked him about the questionable "things Lawson wrote." "I read his book in Britain," one dapper, newly arrived bloke with ruffles stated in dirty Wilmington to him, "and the bloody birds landing on trees could snap the limb right off! I mean really, have

---

[17] Robert Morris became known as the financial backer of the American Revolution. He was a famed English merchant and banker who lived in Philadelphia, PA. He served as a US Senator and was a member of the Continental Congress.

[18] Morristown was renamed Asheville, NC after NC Governor Samuel Ashe in Buncombe County (named after Colonel Edward Buncombe formerly of the island called St. Christopher (today St. Kitts). Buncombe was wounded and captured as Colonel of the 5th NC Regiment at the great battle of Germantown and buried in Philadelphia (after falling down some stairs sleep-walking one night). Ashe was an orphan at the age of nine and became an attorney to the Crown. He served in the militia during the war on the Patriot side and Ashe County as well as Asheboro is named after him. Knowing your history and where you are driving through, or to, is really important. These are things you can share with family and friends.

[19] Hernando shocked people when his mother ships appeared off of Tampa, FL and the "aliens" landed who was from another world. They rode on top of large animals never before seen called caballos (horses). In our state, we would later see Spanish Mustang horses running up and down the beaches at Corolla, near Kitty Hawk. They have been allowed to run free and the tours today in jeeps and modified Humvees are fascinating. The hundreds of armed men traveling with De Soto also "glistened" in the sun and could be seen from 50 miles away when the sun bounced off of their shiny plate armor and helmets if you were a scout atop a mountain. It was eery and scary. Arrows and spears shattered against the plate with no result. And we now know that the first inland European settlement in the United States is no longer Jamestown, VA. It has been correctly replaced with carbon-14 dating and archaeological proof to actually be in North Carolina by Morganton. It is called Fort San Juan named after Captain Juan Pardo. This is 20 years before The Lost Colony, 40 years before Jamestown, and 53 years before the heralded Mayflower landed in Plymouth.

you seen this jackasses words? Do modern educated people expect that we shall believe this level of exaggeration to try and explain the wild new world to us? THIS IS the modern world, my good man."[20]

Private Ishmael Titus couldn't read but knew it was accurate. "I'm sure that with more of the settlers and mores huntings, sirs, someday this will be a thing of the past. I know it's hard to believe for you a comings from a city like the big London."

"Yes, why YES, it is," he sneered.

Having it happen during his lifetime at least nine times no longer scared him. He would have awoken and just rolled over with the thunderous juggernaut violence in the middle of deep sleep. Thinking only, another limb I guess. Oh well. Its what you get used to.

Last night was comical, though. No less than several dozen had hopped up from their luxurious grass beds like idiots, began commotion and yelling, appealing a storm had come, or a cannon went off, lightning from the sky hit the tree and all sorts of childlike ideas. Had these peoples never been in the countryside? Well, it wasn't hogwash my friends, he had thought, this happens now and then. And YES if plentiful birds land on a tree limb, it snaps it right the hell off! But, of course, when he tried to explain it, and there was no need to worry, the "dumb slave" was not believed.

---

[20] Oh, it's the modern world alright, buddy. John Lawson published his A New Voyage to Carolina; Containing the Exact Description and Natural History of That Country: Together with the Present State Thereof. And a Journal of a Thousand Miles, Travel'd Thro' Several Nations of Indians. Giving a Particular Account of Their Customs, Manners, &c. out of London in 1709. He was the Surveyor General Of North Carolina from 1708-1711. There is a historical marker behind the Charlotte Museum of History that is excellent to visit on your way past the large American Freedom Bell. A stop to hear it ring is a lifetime trip on your way up to the Hezekiah Alexander Home. You can read all you want on the web or in books, but you can't smell the inside of that home, or dip your hand into the cold water of the Spring House. The marker reads: John Lawson Surveyor General Of North Carolina, (1708-1711), In 1701 John Lawson (1674-1711), who became Surveyor General of Carolina, traveled along Sugaw Creek after entering North Carolina near Pineville from South Carolina. He came through eastern Mecklenburg County, staying three or four days and spending one day hunting pigeons, which were numerous. His exploratory voyage of more than 500 miles began at Charles Town, SC on December 28, 1700, and ended at Washington, NC, on February 24, 1701. His description of the state in his book, A New Voyage to Carolina, published in 1709, is the most comprehensive for that time period. Marker Placed By The North Carolina Society, Colonial Dames XVII Century, Project Of 2001-2003 State President, Mary Ellen Sloan Hinson.

"Shut up stupid ni**er boy slave that's the British Legion with Colonel Tarleton following us and come to rescue I'll bet," one prisoner gambled.

"It was just a tree breaking apart, and I'm not gonna be a slaves much longer, sir. I sided with the right side and whens we creates the new country I gets my freedom. It's in mys contract with my owner," he proudly warned.

"Well, you could have been free with us also. Why we have freed tens of thousands of slaves all over the colonies. We would sign a paper with you for your freedom assured now if you considered helping us to escape. If you can find some paper and but a quill. Why wait and risk it?" **(Ishmael Titus is featured in the first ever commissioned painting completed in US history – all rights owned by author)**

"No sirs, no sirs, a lobster is best boiled and thens eaten with salted butter we melts in the pot!" Ishmael taunted (featured in the first ever commissioned painting completed in US history by Jeff Trexler – all rights owned by author).

He quickly fired back, "Why if I still had my sword I'd run you through for that you filthy ni**er boy."

"Which is whys I know yous a liar, sir. And a damned liar at that. All you duz is speaks foul to me the whole time we've been marching and I guarding you. If'n ya donts watch your mouth one of them white officers is gonna run you through with his sword ifn I tells him what a jerk you is!"

"Oh you mean like they did yesterday and today, as fucking killers?" he questioned. "When that private tried to escape and was found hiding in a tree? They stabbed him to death inside of the trunk instead of just having him rejoin us as a prisoner!?"

Another piped up to support this line of attack while stretching out his creaked neck, who was formerly lying on the ground and using a somewhat smooth gray rock for his pillow, "Yeah, I saw it all, they killed the poor prisoner and repeatedly stabbed him inside of that dead tree where he had been found hiding – that's a violation of warfare and a war crime – you killers."

Private Titus leveled his Pennsylvania long rifle towards the two of them gripping the excellent hewn wooden barrel with his rough weathered hands and right finger inserted into the brass trigger guard and goaded, "Well why wait then and comes and gets your fate right now with lead buried in your gut sews you can bleed out in the red ant hills of Carolina. Oh dems red ants love the smell of blood round these parts. Only things better is I put a hornet's nest afittin onto your head!" He didn't need to look down to finger probe around and make sure he was ready to cock and fire. He knew what the metal trigger felt like.

A hornet's nest might not be hard to find as a large one was hanging from a tree seen earlier from the trail at around noon in the fall colored forest this time of year of brown, red, green, yellow, and orange leaves.

"That is if your gun even goes off, considering how much rain we've had these past few days.[21] You'd best hope it even works with damp powder, darkie boy. By the time we are on you, we'll inject that stock into your ass and have it come out with your front teeth to taste your own shit. What do you think of that ni**er servant and boot shiner? Would you like to lick your own ass and taste it in your mouth?"

Ishmael mocked back, "Oh nooooo, no, no, no, no sir, now thatsin a tricky you mens had with your paper damp cartridges. I fills my beast from the horn dry, with excellent powder, as a parched throat on a sunny day with no waters found for miles. And we've got the most beautiful powder in the colonies made with woman power to the rescue! That's been one of our fun little secrets is beating you lobster boys with our women at all of these battles!

"You boys was beaten by titties on a girl!" shouted another guard, Michael, in full brown one-piece linen hunting frock moving over to support Ishmael, pointing his long rifle frighteningly. "Hows about some fresh squeeze milk in the face now, Lil' babies?"

Captain Carr of Georgia, a patriot, was now within earshot. "Why don't you stop that kind of inappropriate talk. No one wants to hear that type of filthy language laced with childish jokes we told as boys. And act like a grown fucking man."

"Well she's just getting rich anyway all around here off of your backs by charging robbery prices for it and promoting terror like the psychological deviant she is," a third English prisoner, Captain Walter Gilkey, interjected. "We've heard all about her, your secret Mary, and she's a charlatan and war profiteer only interested in the silver coin offered to Judas.

"Shut all of your mouths!," fired Captain Carr.

---

[21] This was a major tactical complaint from the battle on the British side in that their paper cartridges in leather belt boxes were slightly moist and experienced dampened firepower, blast, and ignition problems due to days of rain. However, the Patriots side was noted for having a super dry powder that was finely made and sounded like individual cannons going off. It's not uncommon to overload in the heat of battle to provide massive, killing power blasts into the enemy. This does run the risk of having your rifle explode into your own face or body, but some don't care. Especially in the heat of battle. That rain had also tactically concealed usually crunching leaves as the rebels surrounded the British.

Gilkey went on, "You rebels have it all wrong and in so many ways of lies, fraud, and disgrace."

Titus stood firm and towered over them there sitting in the solid rocks and green grass, his gray flax-made britches clad legs spread apart in dominance with grubby, leather smelling socks worn five weeks without being washed in tarnished buckle shoes, "Now this ni**er boy slave as you likes to call me is actually a full grown man who once saved Colonel Cleaveland's life so let me puts you in yo place. Folks is agitated and starving an that wasn't right to kill that boy with a sword in the tree. But I didnst doos that. And while yo runnin your mouth, our lady hero Mary Patton DONATED that 500 pounds of black powder for free to whip yo asses at the battle of King's Mountain! An that's the real truth of British lies, fraud, and disgrace. An I heards what ya saids in the disgrace of Gods eyes about us, about your offer, and about me."

The private court of privates had been adjudicated.

Chapter 4: The daily work of a "deviant and rebel," Mary Patton

For every reason when the husband of Mary, John Patton, made tea in the afternoon, it was the tender signal to her that it was afternoon delight that day.

The sun would shine in as the branches swayed in light wind on perfect days early. Avoiding the need for candles. He would always bake scones for her and have them on the heavy round table of iron straps screwed together with hickory[22] with smaller flowers he had picked on a plate nearing death within two hours unless she gave them to water. His plucking was only a minute before his calling for her each time. Why didn't he ever pick large ones or longer ones, she often mused. It's just one of his little ways.

Being raised with scones, singing specific songs while churning butter,[23] and jam, Mary remembered these traditions of her family despite leaving the UK isles at an early age. Which is why John used such beautiful thin-handled cups and matching green flowered china[24] saucers that they kept safely on the cupboard. A rare luxury for people living in the backwoods of the forbidden zone.

---

[22] A prized wood today as it generally costs more to purchase a solid hickory piece of furniture. Especially with so many particle board items for sale that include CAM locks and putting it all together for hours at your house.

[23]. Butter churning songs are viral in this period and culturally oriented. They are famed from country to country and colony to colony.

[24] The word china is not new on earth, as a country, but Samuel Johnson includes it as porcelain in his two-volume dictionary set - shattering records worldwide, in 1755. That was because "china" was invented in China. Makes sense, eh? I know you may think I'm a bit whacko, but I just love this kind of history. The language of English, by this time, was in a critical phase of needing a REAL dictionary to use on earth. Johnson was approached by several printers in London to help fix the problem and took several years to perfect it. Plates, cups, and bowls were just decided to be called "china" in the English language. As this is a book and not an academic paper, I typically offer my bibliography. I am well known as an expert in citation and references for my university studies and provide it here. Johnson, S. (1755). A Dictionary of the English Language... to Which are Prefixed a History of the Language, and an English Grammar. 2 vols. The BBC has a terrific documentary on Johnson you can watch on your smartphone or tablet, and while his actual dictionary can be bought for $1500.00 from antique dealers, it is fun to look up words in the 1700s via the online version.

As soon as she came in, he was smiling and grinning so she took her scarf off and hat laughing, "Oh is it time for that then?" And she sauntered over and held him in her arms to look upon his face and coax back his hair with her right hand.

"It tis my love and if we were in a factory, on a croppers farm or in an office we could never enjoy ourselves as we do owning our own business!" John Patton giggled and swayed his wife back and forth in silliness with her still encapsulating his arms inside of hers. It was awkward but silly just the same – as resembled their affection.

Mary took his hand to the bedroom leading him first as any bold woman would do if she felt like it. And she felt like it. Because she deeply loved him with all of her heart and soul. Body and mind were just actors in their drama doing what their spirits ordered as if mere subjects in the kingdom of their majestic palace. Inside of their darling and honey was a vast castle impregnable by any human forces, laws, rules, Sheriffs, Judges, or wars. And he liked how that felt. To have her lead and take the initiative at times since it relieved the pressure on him to always start and perform, and to risk rejection. Which was hardly ever in the safety of their risks on the back trails and kindness in their care for one another.

They had come to intimacy long ago in the peacefulness of open conversation about what they enjoyed, how they liked it, and what didn't work. They had been told this was the secret to intimacy and productive, talkative marriages. Nothing was secretive about positions, acts, doing things differently. At the ten year mark of making love, everything had still been evolving in the security of their secrets held by hearts entwined in one white silk bow. Spanking for one another, tickling for one another, licking of each other, titillating was not just for only one of them and their nipples to be made hard with the swirl of a wet tongue.

They enjoyed making love and were bound as the dove is to the purity of Christ to one another. And it remained hot and torrid trying to achieve a dozen children. Which was believed fruitless in accomplishment but a grade of A for trying. Yet Mary and John both knew no one would ever know about what they did with one another. It was their private and secret world as lovers.

They had no desire to break that bond and held each other gaze in laughter from across a room, a field, or pressed into each other's arms – anytime, and anywhere.

No interloper held any regard for their common allegiance. From the bristling young men that were employees with thick biceps and had torn open ribcages that resembled a hard metal washboard when the sweaty shirt was free. To the succulent young ladies with large breasts and tight waists shrouded in freshly washed and long golden hair that reached down to the buttock length.

John and Mary could care less.

There were still days in the sunlight and broad open daisies of the hillside that they went at it, and nights found in the barn bent over with dress pulled up amongst prickly hay that stuck you with a memory for a week of jokes.

All one had to do was mention, "Hey, hay!?" And private, embarrassing laughter would ensue.

Nothing was ever filthy. And everything they did was always beautiful for them. After all, they felt, we are a married couple, and in God's eyes, we are devout.

"What's so funny, amongst you two, this time?" a customer and friend John Sevier[25] had once asked.

"Oh, it's just another one of our private jokes, John," Mary laughed aloud to relieve some of the tension and slight embarrassment in the air.

"Well, it gets weird around here at times when you two start the laughter up like that again. Makes a fellow wonder if its something he did or just doesn't get the joke he hadn't heard yet."

John Patton came over and slapped him on the back. "Now Colonel Sevier, you know we moved down here from Pennsylvania with love in our hearts for everything the settlement is

---

[25]. Colonel John Sevier and later, Governor Sevier. A former innkeeper, or B&B operator in Virginia, like his father.

doing, and we are in love with one another and have our private moments. It's been our joy to see the war end and the Confederacy[26] do so well."

"Yes, it certainly has and if only Mary were as famous as Captain Molly for all she did!" Sevier noted.[27]

Mary mentioned, "It's okay. I remember when she first moved to our town of Carlisle in the Pennsylvania colony. Her family were so nice and widely accepted into the community. It was right as we were moving down South ourselves.[28] She was such a nice person and resolute like me. We helped one another – her moving in and I moving South. I wasn't surprised at all to hear of her brazen fame in battle."

Such were the days of work together on the farm and in their black powder operation. Aside from interruptions (of their own making) they had customers who dropped by like Sevier, the Taylor's, Hyder's, and Carter's to name just a few of the thousands in the region.

The work was dangerous and hot during the long summers. Just as much, operations continued in the winter and could be freezing at times limiting work hours. The cold weather also elongated saltpeter production – one of three ingredients needed for black powder.

---

[26] The United States of America first operated as a confederation until 1789 and was referred to as a confederacy in writing and the spoken word. Most people think the confederacy was during the Civil War. Once apprised and they start digging around, they find excellent reading as historians.

[27] "Captain Molly," later became known in history as the famed, alleged, mythical Molly Pitcher. At first, writings about her feats and prints sold as such. Her name was actually Mary Ludwig Hays McCauly, and her husband was artilleryman William Hays. She is legendary during the American Revolutionary War for carrying water to soldiers, cooling cannons with it and taking over when her husband was injured working the cannon at the battle of Monmouth, NJ. As no photographs or evidence-based proof submitted to a court existed some scholars sought to smear and denigrate her shero work in combat as a woman. Then, in 1822, based on her legal and binding application for a widow's pension the State of Pennsylvania awarded her an annual grant and Hay's military record was verified. Today, one can find monuments dedicated to her contributions during the war at her hometown of Carlisle, PA and at the battlefield.

[28] This was in fact about the time that the Patton's packed up and headed over the mountains to live in North Carolina sometime between the 1774 to 1780 timeframe. Mary McKeehan was born in 1751 in England, immigrated to the Colonies in the late 1760s, married Irish immigrant John Patton in 1772 and passed away in 1836. It is important to note on maps of this time that the North Carolina extends all the way to the Mississippi River. It would not be cut in half to create the new State of Franklin until 1784/5, and later the more modern State called Tennessee in 1796.

Each night, Mary's beloved John would take his brass-buckled shoes off and place them in the corner of the living and kitchen area of their cabin home. It was as if they had their own little overnight grave there. **(Mary is featured here in the first ever commissioned painting completed in US history by Jeff Trexler – all rights owned by author)** They carried the stink of the days work as John's feet suffered from extreme pains unknown as to why. He was the only one allowed to have shoes on around the house. Everyone else left there's outside.

During the day the children would help.

"Mother," eldest Margaret would ask, "What shall we work on today and this week with the children?"

Mary would direct the entire team during breakfast today of natural eggs, ham slices cooked on the flat black iron in the fireplace slightly charred on the left including any helpers hired through John and Margaret. The ham got blackened by accident. If schooling were planned in the home or at the wooden church, they would work around that. Learning and practicing a trade was always much more critical in this area. Especially ones like this involving science and crystal making.[29] Even with Reverend Samuel Doak establishing his school in Jonesborough that he named the Martin Academy in 1783, it still was a five-hour walk one way or a long two-hour ride **one way** by horse or carriage.

"It's just too long to try and bring them there each day," John would complain as part of his final push in a long-running debate.

"Well it's the first school ever west of the mountains, John, and their education is essential. We can't work them to death all day here like we do ourselves."

"I'm sure if we have business in Jonesborough that day they can all attend in their finest clothes and we will pick them up after. Just like the city folk does daily."

And that's how that conversation had gone. Sending them, there was a luxury item engaged in infrequently – even though highly regarded. Therefore lots of help would work the gunpowder mill daily.

Mary instructed Margaret, "I was thinking this week we will spend four days grinding charcoal in the mill as we need so much of it for the next master batch, on the chart that will be MB 899. And then we will visit the darkness on Friday and Saturday to see our friends and

---

[29] The process Mary was taught in the UK is a slow one - of three ingredients, 1. saltpeter or potassium nitrate, 2. sulfur, and 3. charcoal. The crystal making portion of saltpeter/potassium nitrate is the more challenging one. Being safe means grinding each one on specific days and only working in a fire safe area, keeping the ingredients apart from one another until mixed at the very end. Mixing with a wooden dowel is a lot smarter than using metal objects to keep down on static electricity or discharge. A robust wooden mortar and log pestle work also. A lot of gunpowder mills exploded in the old days in a plume of fire and smoke that arched into the blue sky – you knew the family over yonder just went up.

collect." The darkness was Mary's secret map listing of 17 bat caves[30] she had around the area for 50 miles where they collected bat drippings or poop to make nitre.[31] "Batch 14 of the Nitre[32] is going well with excellent crystals, and then we can look at the other batches."

John would be busy working in various buildings of the factory compound. "We have some items I'm working on to repair, rebuild, and three parts I am going to replace, Mary. I may need to go underwater also just to look at part of the wheel flow and currents, and we are strengthening the dam by the other side," he updated her. Everyone knew about their mill and the wheel turning to create a fine powder on the market as was the famous Swiss and French powders. The final mix drew from their supplies and would change depending on pistol, rifle, musket, or cannon powder made. An essential blend was 75% nitre (saltpeter or potassium nitrate), 15% charcoal, and 10% sulfur. The powder was always milled, stamped, or crushed with a forgotten and fourth ingredient, water, to keep it wet and safe until dried out later.

---

[30] Many of us authors and historians casually call Mary "Batwoman" – like Claire Fraser in Outlander, who wore a bat cape and outfit. The two are excellent Sheroes for all to emulate. It is not exactly certain how many caves she had in total. It could possibly be more.

[31] Also called guano, if you want to get all scientific and sound smart. Hardly any gunpowder was made in the colonies at the time of the war so ramping up fecal collection became very important. The Continental Congress printed pamphlets on how to collect and deliver niter/nitre to Philadelphia as far away as the SC colony. Guano was one of the best sources of making nitre (saltpeter or potassium nitrate).

[32] Nitre was not actually scientifically understood like it is today.

Chapter 5: Winning the war and becoming a wealthy landowner

Mary and John listened to the Taylor's for a good two hours that night in their peaceful home of Carlisle, PA, about becoming rich, moving their whole family, selling their business for hard cash, taking the two girls out of school, and departing the church.

The candles flickered in pretty tin holders, and the light was mirrored by the glass. Groaning stomachs hungry before and moaning stuffed after. Smoke had been blown down the chimney for a half minute enough to open the doors and air out those wooden walls. Black padlock on a muscular wood chest seen in the bedroom by the foot of the bed. Dry grass tracked in on the floor to be angrily swept out later with the fury of aggressive cleaning and living in a city home. Actual three-tine forks – relative obscurity to use the fork.[33] A stain was on the floor of possibly strong tea, coffee, or something, that couldn't be scrubbed out and likewise on the table, twice in the shapes of clouds. The first time it happens you curse under your breath but then realize stains are often permanent in this life. You can't take a table down to the river and beat it with a rock to get the stain out.[34]

The pewter, clay, and porcelain plates. Although mixed, added charm.

They had fresh water in a pitcher and a china wash basin with a real cotton towel to even wipe your face with.

All the Taylor's down South had was flax and linen items in their homes. The richness of it all impressed many, and if you needed more water, it could easily be had and quickly. Some of the shops in town seen that day had the actual glass, see-through windows you could look into - and see sausages and cheeses hanging. It was a reminder of what could be mesmerizing in Philadelphia or New York.

---

[33] The fork is not as popular as many thought in colonial America. Few use it just yet.
[34] And you were thinking about spraying it with something and getting some paper towels out?

The local church struck its bell and people knew what time it was. And that was a fantastic shock to watch John take a pocket watch out and adjust the time throughout the day. It was as if he had a fixation with his handheld wonder he carried everywhere or couldn't do without.[35] His link to the world in his hands.

No bells were striking in the wilderness reminding folks what time it was where they were from in the Watauga Association of Western North Carolina.

A pole hammered into the ground helped tell precisely when it was noon and observing the shadow compass; otherwise, you worked as long and hard as you could daily and into the pitch black darkness. You could check the time at the top of a mountain the same way with a stick.

You often would guess at what time it was and you realized visitors to Western North Carolina[36] gave up on their watches and winding with nothing to compare them to - like the local clock tower – after a few days they became unreliable. So you might work into the night! Unlike Carlisle, where folks immediately ceased work around five and "had to get home for dinner."

What a childish notion, you could have dinner and keep working standing up with a biscuit or cooked ear of corn in a pocket that had gotten cold three hours ago and then a damned apple for dessert.

But Ann, nor Andrew Taylor, wanted to push it or say those things out loud. They realized quickly how asinine their position and proposal to John and Mary was coming off.

This might actually take a few days of convincing talk.

---

[35] Now this may sound familiar to you regarding a smart phone...
[36] Sometimes called the Republic of Watauga and later became the Washington District and the Washington County of North Carolina loyal to the United Colonies. After that, the area would develop into The State of Franklin or the Free Republic of Franklin or the State of Frankland. Franklin's first capital was Jonesborough, and that needs to be on your Tennessee bucket list of magical colonial places to admire and visit. Later came Lesser Franklin, the Southwest Territory, and finally becoming the state of Tennessee.

It was a lot to take in after they had prepared a nice dinner of cock-a-leekie soup,[37] cottage pie,[38] shepherds pie, colcannon and clapshot,[39] soda bread, bannocks,[40] handmade shortbread for dessert and fresh berry trifle – they had gone all out to host their dear friends.

Mary and John often made the shepherds pie with the lamb and the cottage pie with the ground beef. These recipes were cousins. The cottage pie recipe was a legend. It uses 3 1/2 lbs of ground meat cooked off in the oven - set aside to cool, pour off the fat into gravy pan, as it is beefy flavored and can be used for a roux (French code for thickener). The had also made this recipe with ground bison, and ground buffalo which are popular and plentiful.

Then, 4 carrots, 5 celery stalks, 1 large onion, diced, then sauteed to a tender state and set aside to cool - or roast on a pan set inside a dutch oven about an hour with a little olive oil and toss around once in a while with a spatula.

FOR THE GRAVY: Salt and pepper to taste, a splash of wine (about 1/2 a cup), 5 tbsp tomato paste, 1/2 cup strong beef bullion (or so), 1/2 cup of drained off beef fat and a tad of flour to make a simple gravy. Combine the beef fat (and possibly a stick of salted butter) with plain flour to make your paste[41] and cook until dark brown[42] (roux) and then add the wine,

---

[37] Today this remains as the Scottish National Soup adored worldwide. It was on the menu the day the Titanic went down and considered fancy. It most likely came from France and used onions initially – we Scottish changed it to leeks. It first appeared in a cookbook in 1598. You may find it most proudly served in Edinburgh, Scotland and it also goes by Cock a Leeky or Auld Reeky (Old Reeky).

[38] Usage of the tomato is a contentious item. After the tomato comes to Europe and is eaten and planted, I detect from 1770 forward the use of tomato. One must be mindful that Italians never knew of nor ate tomatoes in the history of the country. The pizzas that we hand make from 400 BC are definitely different. In cottage pie, tomato flavors the ground beef. It's a terrific inclusion! So the truth of Cottage Pie is that it changed over the years - think about it being made before having tomato paste. Depending on your authentic Scottish guest visiting you in America, you may ask about true Scottish cuisine and would they like the "pre-1770 Cottage Pie, or after the tomato comes to Europe version?" Some of the facts I present are based on knowing how to prepare authentic foods based on science and history. This is my family's version served at Scottish dinners and for Outlander events.

[39] These are two famous Irish and Scottish mashed potato dishes that we make and serve often! Clapshot is more so Scottish.

[40] These are like scones and found on the table at all three meals daily.

[41] You can also just use Wondra flour today and enjoy more modern cooking if you like. It also speeds up the process.

[42] In recent times we chefs use Kitchen Bouquet – a darkening aromatic liquid.

tomato paste, and beef bouillon (strong broth). Thin, more or less, with hot water or even more broth to your gravy flavor liking;[43] to make your version and dump in the ground beef.

Mix all other items together and put into a crock with 9 strands of fresh thyme stripped and added to the final mix. Throw the stems away.

FOR THE MASHED POTATO TOPPING: Top with a simple combination of mashed potatoes (butter, milk, shredded extra-sharp cheddar, 1 t pumpkin pie spice (optional)). Bake at 425 degrees for up to an hour. You can broil if you like to brown or decorate it with a small amount of cheddar cheese, or butter pats.

They enjoyed cooking together, and the food was an enjoyable part of their lives. Like anyone, it also represented their culture and customs. But mainly that of Scotch-Irish family recipes and lore.

Their decision to move down South was decided to be reflected on for that evening, and an answer is given in a few days. The presentation had seemed a strong push for them to do so and Ann had explained this was the perfect storm of events that made so much sense.[44]

"On the one hand, we believe there are at least 5,000 caves present to obtain bat dung from[45] and produce a diamond-level black powder with it," Andrew digressed. "And you know when it comes to nitre how desperate the colonies and General Washington are.

"The bat does make a superior waste in my opinion," agreed Mary.

---

[43] We also often add four or five shakes of Worcestershire sauce in our modern classes but realize this was not invented in Worcester until 1835, around Mary's passing to her second life. John had left around 1808 to go on to eternal life. Worcestershire sauce is a highly fermented barrel condiment created in the city named Worcester. It is in a shire called Worcestershire of England. The experimental chemists were John Wheeley **Lea &** William Henry **Perrins**.

[44] No author or research completed has ever analyzed the historic combination of US Geological Survey deposits for sulfur, scientific investigation of Eastern Tennessee cave patterns of bats and guano, and the combination of water power before this book. All authors on earth have previously only mentioned the basic facts about that have been regurgitated for hundreds of years and adding nothing to the real truth of the perfect storm.

[45] There are over 10,000 caves in the state of Tennessee, and one recently was counted nearby the Patton Blackpowder Factory to have just over 85,000 bats in it. JCPress. (2019). Big bat cave population surveyed in East Tennessee. Retrieved from http://www.johnsoncitypress.com/Environment/2017/02/23/Big-bat-cave-population-surveyed-in-East-Tennessee

John added, "With hardly anyone living down where you are on the other side of the mountain – it causes me grave concern. Where would we get all of the outhouse crap from, you've hardly anyone there – and that also means few to little animals dropping their loads."

Andrew replied his intelligent findings stoutly, "Wagons of crap and outhouse trays emptied are arriving at the black powder mills all around New Jersey and Philadelphia. Congress is printing pamphlets on the whole process and all wagons from as far away as South Carolina are directed in an emergency-like manner to bring the shate to them."

John argued now, "Then where do we fit in as supposedly becoming rich when we use the makings of the poop as 75% of our black powder!? We need so much of it, and you will certainly have little to nothing down there.

"And you want us to avoid the impending British invasion of Pennsylvania by leaving our comfortable home to go and live in the wilderness, subject to constant Indian attack?" Mary threw in. "I've read the little girls run wild naked until reaching puberty and that men or women are allowed to walk out of their marriages anytime they like – besides killing whites and scalping us they have some strange customs that we do not agree with."

"Let me explain a few more parts of the story to you of this unique region and why I believe you would cash in," Andrew encouraged. "The things you just said about the Indians are actually about the Catawba's by Charlottetown, and they are the best around as friends of the Patriots. They are helping us, unlike the Cherokee who are against us and with the Tories."

"But how can they legally allow a man, or a woman, to leave a marriage for no reason? Or for nude children to run free in the fields? These are things we are deeply against in our faith and God's eyes. AND I DON'T WANT TO SEE NUDE GIRLS WALKING AROUND."

"They are different and do that in their own area and towns. Like the many religions moving to the new world, we are all different. We all respect one another's beliefs as long as it doesn't involve religious oppression or killing people like the British presently do. And besides, the divorce laws the Catawba Indians have only allow for that once a year – it's a big thing they dance to during their Green Corn Ceremony.[46] You will meet their women leaders who control the towns, corn, beans, squash, and gourd fields and own businesses just like yourself, Mary!"

Mary seemed surprised, "They have women who own companies like me?"

"Yes they do, Mary. They are quite different, and also enjoy cooking like you and John" Andrew shared. He seemed to have gotten her on the hook with this one. "Why they even run whole peach orchards."

Ann Taylor comforted, "I know moving from Pennsylvania to the wilderness will be good for you in the peacefulness of your own farm, John and Mary – not to mention expanding your black powder company and factory mill." And she reached and took Mary's hand in her own and patted the top of it.

"I love fresh peaches – can you imagine a whole basket?" John blurted out, and Mary slant eyed him. He could tell she didn't like most of what she was hearing.

"Well, they also already run their worlds like our new proposals to get rid of King George and having one person making decisions. Decisions in the Catawba peoples government are made by consensus, and the leader is commonly not permitted to decide alone what will happen. They will be a good neighbor and guide for our own dreams of running America." Ann tried to add in.

Mary stood up and walked over to stoke the fire. It was burning low, and she put some more small brushwood in to crank it up again and then another log on top of that to bring them into the night. "I know we undertook to meet and exchange for several days about this idea of

---

[46] During the Green Corn Ceremony, married men or women may leave the spouse of their own free will and without providing reasons to be adjudicated by any court tribunal. If a man then married a divorced woman he had to reimburse the previous husband for any gifts, goods, or animals equivalent to what the former husband had given at her first wedding. While the Catawba people loved making turtle stew with "kaya" (river turtle) they also used leftover parts of the kaya to make the ceremonial dress look fancy and built shell rattles for use during the ceremony. Sally New River would later teach Mary how they roasted acorns and used the nut meat inside to thicken deer soup.

yours, but I can't say that I am very hopeful. If I had to decide tonight my answer would be no thank you."

They met the next day again to listen to more of the proposal and promises of financial support, but the answer was decided not to move from Carlisle. Even when Taylor's deflected questions about immigration rules amongst the Indian nations they remained concerned during talks of day three.

"It has been a pleasure," John beamed, "to dine in a tavern with us four just for lunch – can you imagine, us taking our lunch out and paying for it in the woods?"

"Well, no, not really John," Andrew teased, "But we do request one another over and make lunch for free for each family!"

They all laughed aloud, and John seemed to laugh the hardest and into his own face. He didn't mind laughing at himself. Andrew was right.

"But, I have meant to bring up to you the issue of immigration in America and the borders. More and more are coming every day. What are all of the Indians saying and deciding?" Mary questioned.

"It's the same thing since they own all of the lands and are in charge. His flatulence, King of the Britons, has even said we are not allowed to live on the other side of the mountain," Ann threatened. "But Valentine[47] and his son, John, won't take that laying down!"

"Best to keep your voice down – that's a crime they are allowed to execute you over," Mary warned her.

Andrew picked it up where his wife Ann had left off, "We have bought and paid for what they want to sell us - or lease to us. We try to get a long lease whenever possible. The majority

---

[47] Valentine Sevier, Sr. was a famous B&B host – in those days an inn was called a tavern. His son, who lived in the Watauga Association area had also tried his hand at heads in beds with service of tankards of ale - but didn't care for it. Later he would become the famous Colonel John Sevier at the Battle of Kings Mountain, Governor of the state of Franklin and the first Governor of Tennessee. He holds the unique distinction of being a Governor of two states.

of them at many of their great gatherings have decided to continue to allow immigration to occur in America," they both explained.

John had one final question, "And when Washington switched sides and showed up in his new, blue uniform, where many of them angered he was not with the British Army any longer?"

"That's true," Ann retorted, "but they were not angered. Many were confused and mentioned he looked like he had simply turned his red uniform inside out and now had a blue jacket on with red cuffs and lapels. Honestly, and secretly, some of the Indians laughed at it when they first saw him." She took a final sip from her now cold teacup. It could be a long time since she sat in a tavern such as this again. Best to drink it all in.

At the close of the fourth day of their stay, the Taylor's, despite being good friends - were sent back home in disappointment. They had recruited two other families. But not the Patton's and certainly not to sell their powder operation and leave their home and town.

Mary cried and hugged Ann and gave notice for her to bid her well wishes to her sisters memory, Elizabeth Wilson Taylor[48] "when you next see her, and I am so sorry our answer has been long, it has been a resounding NO, and not to your liking. But we love thee dearest friends, we love thee and thine."

So what if they were not going to become wealthy landowners. No one really cares, Mary thought to herself.

---

[48] When Andrew Taylor loses his loving wife Elizabeth, he actually later marries her sister, Ann until he himself passes away in 1787. The Taylors have a long and powerful legacy in America as Governors, a President, General, and Senator.

Chapter 6: The family today, a family of love

My great-great-great grandfather's buckle shoes sat on the floor covered in endless torrents of silent dust for decades. Since I was 14 those leather, black friends had been told to me of his life and deeds in times fraught with war and hardships from 1775-1783. However, no one ever moved them, so there they remained with us all as "pop-pop in the corner," pop-pop with us somehow and staring or listening or thinking. He was always here.

In the 1800s, the colossal cabin home settled and some jacking was done as men worked on the foundation, but grandpop never moved. It was a well-known sin to even touch the iron buckles with the bump of the dustpan or sweep of the broom. Although no one ever had told me THAT or said it... We just all knew it.

After the turn of the century it WAS brought up (the subject) at Thanksgiving in 1927, Jim Bob unsettled the whole dinner table and made family lore passed on to each of our generations as sacred history. He broached the subject.

"How could you even think of touching them," angered Mary to him as we sat with gaping mouths. For my part, I know I showed chewed stuffing in my open maw, so closed it quickly. Johnathan dropped his fork and mother looked extremely concerned.

"I just was reading that a leather treatment would help preserve antique goods and"

Momma interrupted, "This is not the type of thing to ruin a Thanksgiving over, Jim Bob, and you should know better!"

The shocking part wasn't Jim Bob's ideas so much, I mean really (our family acts as if this is the blasphemer raised up out of a coffin of the graveyard, Satanic proportions over these shoes), or what he had read about or even mothers interjection. It was what came next, the holy presence of the mountain man BEING NOW FORCED TO STOP EATING his roast fowl. And that my friends are at times, the worst offense one could commit...

At six-foot-four, feet tall my father weighs in close to 350 pounds of stable packed weight. I think his beard alone is close to four of those pounds. He raised his paw under the power of a bicep the size of my thigh with intimidating fork in hand pointing directly at him (you know who) as the congregation silenced each activity in the pews of chewing, cutting turkey, drinking - not even a gulp could be heard.

There was the anticipation of the Pope's words, and some did breath, or at least that was the only sound could be found. The metal was in his silent hand pointing like a dagger, and the fire in his eyes hung like the darkness of war enacted. No words came. His Holiness didn't need to speak to threaten the crusades of millions to die.

His twin lasers bore through Jim Bob menacing his quiet into capitulation. I think we might have all sat staring at the four tines of that fork for two straight minutes, gripped in the fear his previous combat experience and the things he had seen in modern wars. Certainly the man would not hurt one of his own children with his hands. Would he? At the two minute and one-second mark came the harsh reality of the filthy mouthed rudeness learned in the military shocking all of us with what daddy had experienced. He was going to speak. Or bark fire, flame, and napalm. Now, THIS could fricking ruin the entire holiday dinner. The part of his life and mind no one ever knew of in killing for a living and the part you did not want to ever see, let alone hear. Whatever he had done with weapons and knives in those days were things only seen on the silver screen, and those were gore and violence movies that only boys liked anyway.

"You may be 46 years old boy, but I will bare rump spank you over my knee after I kick your rear around this property into a fine and withered condition. And the shame, indignity, and embarrassment of your father committing this act at your 46 dumb years old will ripple across our church and community into your employer's lunchroom when Momma orders you to never come back here to touch shoes or cranberry sauce for as long as you exist amongst the humans on earth. In fact, if you don't cease these notions to ever mention those shoes again the next time you enter my home will be after putting me into a pine box and throwing dirt on top of me."

Holy heck, this holiday was history! And Jim Bob was in so much trouble, and I mean with Daddy and everyone.

Until he flashed that fork in a circle.

"And all you other attendees of the reading of my and yo Mommas will," (oh no, Jim Bob now had all of us involved in his mess). "Are we clear on the shoes?" daddy threatened.

When my father passed away in 1946 after the second war(s), we were reminded from the pulpit through Jim Bobs crying of "I LOVE Y'ALL."

Although the shoes were not allowed to be mentioned, nor Daddy's hard comments-the last thing father had said before reconvening his eating of the bird was, "now don't forget - I LOVE Y'ALL."

The tears streaming down faces amongst all of my brothers and sisters was enough to recall his terror - and love. For there had been no hugs allowed as we said goodbye on Sunday leaving for our own homes and departing the large cabin.

At least one of us had mentioned, "well he can kiss my ass acting like that, and I can use that word out here on the grass, I ain't inside his house no more."

"I heard that boy, now you go think about what I says bout' dem dirty shoes," came from the porch. Oh my God git going before he comes off of there. And away we all went, hugless,[49] loveless, cast-out in our different colored cars down a driveway with our bewildered spouses and speechless young children.

The log-hewn lodge continues to be shared as a vacation spot by our ever-growing family in the past years. Who is there for two weeks or just a weekend respite is pretty much no longer organized by phone? Instead, we have a private area on Facebook that everyone uses to "reserve." The cobwebs, caked filthy dust and brittle, destroyed American artifact rightfully should have been donated to the museums in Charlotte long ago.

Yet, there they are still untouched on earth and worn by a person few of us were ever impacted by, talked with, met or know much about at all. Now, "our infants," try to get near with a tap on the hand or behind as they grow. "No, no sweetie, those are pop-pops, now you stay away," I warn.

"Who's pop-pop and his shoes dirty, Momma?"

---

[49] Most likely not a real word but it sure seemed to fit the way we felt. Wrong. Wronged. In trouble.

Chapter 7: My grandchildren do not have the same accent as I

Frederick Hambright,[50] a former Colonel at the battle of King's Mountain and family friend, was waiting to come across Mary as she headed down to Charlestown.

They were meeting at a good Irish families stopping point, Michael Gaffney's crossroads and tavern in the upcountry part of South Carolina. Frederick had been waiting with his wife, Mary Dover Hambright, to purchase 48 pounds of powder for many families all around King's Mountain where they still lived at its foot and base. They often would ride down on assigned meeting agreement days and reminisce about the great war, revolution, and following the French revolution. By correspondence, today was the agreed upon day. Currently, they would surely discuss the new war with England. The Second American War of Independence.[51]

Michael's wife Polly[52] was always so nice and came by, "Do you have everything you need Colonel and Mary?" she winked and smiled at Mary. "Michael wants to come back from the store and see you also, ya know and give him some time to come back. He's making bricks and selling those also now!"

"Yes, we have always admired the fine brick chimney. It is quite picturesque to see, Polly, as we come upon the town here. Will you have your house painted someday on a canvas?" Mary pondered.

"It does seem like a fine idea. But will you two stay tonight and go to the springs, the Limestone Springs? There's still talk of building a huge resort for the limestone enjoyment and health."

"I'm not sure. It depends on the menu tonight I think. We might eat and then stay!" Mary hoped to convince Fred (that was her pet name for him) to stay over. And Polly could see it

---

[50] Also Hamprecht and Hambrecht from Bavaria.
[51] Today this is called the War of 1812.
[52] This is Mary Smith of upstate South Carolina– she had a nickname of Polly.

in her hopeful eyes. Well, this was going to take a Prussian dinner to convince him, and maybe one other idea would have the Colonel spend his money at their tavern.

"Well Colonel, what do you think? I was going to make homemade Spaetzle pushed through the colander with my own hands and Sauerbraten just the way your momma used to do it. And you said my cookin' is even better than Mrs. Captain Cook's Tavern in Charlotte!"

"Ya, mine mutter, Got bless her heart. Undt you zink you canst compete vit mine mutter!?" he kidded her and intimidated her.

"No, but there is also cock-fighting tonight at 8 pm, and I know you love to bet and see the latest competitors! Big Roost is going to be in and Silver Tail from Thickety Creek, as well as a half dozen new contenders!"

"Now you have done it, vee must stay. Mary, mine favorite is Silver Tail! Can vee stay now zen, Mary?" The women just looked at one another and giggled inside their secret minds and sixth sense. He hadn't wanted to stay and like most men preferred to whip the horse forward and just go back home to that log cabin of dulldom and boringcastle. But they had turned the tables on him now, and he thought it was his silly idea to stay. "Oh, men, the perfect plan we always said!" as they laughed in the privacy of the kitchen later with one another.

Tonight would be his favorite dinner, his enjoyable cockfighting games with the others, and then secret time in the rented room under the covers with the iron barrel bolt shut tight on the heavy framed door. And women in these parts went to the fights also! But Mary wouldn't be going. She wanted to get ready for his return.

Mary was planning her own version of gambling when he came back. But there would only be one cock that was fighting in the round arena tonight with just two betters allowed in. She had a system of bookmaking with Fred on how long he would last. He rarely won. He had 22 children between his previous wife (12 with Sarah Hardin) and her (10 more), and she made him pay her in coin. No one has ever known the truth about it except a very few ladies like Polly, who they told each other everything. And then, but very rarely would she allow him to pay his debts between her legs with his tongue to taste and tickle her. It wasn't that she

didn't love that. It was about letting him off the hook without paying up in real money.[53] She was younger than him and had secretly packed a new piece of clothing she had bought. What a night it would be. But he didn't know about the French Negligee[54] imported all the way down from New York and across the ocean from Paris. That was a surprise for the love of her life. Her Fred.

"And then, when you brought up tonights fights, I knew he was done!" Mary laughed with Polly to the point where she covered her own mouth and caught the slightest amount of spittle in her hand to wipe on her dress casually so Polly wouldn't see.

(Colonel Frederick Hambright is featured here in the first ever commissioned painting completed in US history – all rights owned by author). The rains had soaked the dry roads into a muddy, brown mess of ruts, slop, and puddles. Dead carpenter bees had given up the battle and could be seen on the Spring ground too often meaning they had come out early thinking it was safe. It wasn't

---

[53] I have little to nothing to say or add.
[54] From the French language this word gives one the wrong idea, literally 'given little thought or attention', and the feminine past participle of négliger - to neglect. Well there would be no neglect later that night.

safe yet. Why slushy sleet and soft snow had cheered many children that day with the tease of tomorrow off or early dismissal as The matriarch of the Patton family wandered in her memories out the windows.

"But vaht vaas it Mary zat changed your undt mind? Ven zey Taylor's came back through, zey were so disappointed that you and John had said nine, you said no. Zey Taylor's were crushed. And zen, you move down anyway?" Frederick asked after she had come in and gotten herself seated and settled with her grandson. He went back out the muddy door to tend to the horses. "I hast been meaning to ask you zees for such a long time," he added. Polly had already served all three of them, and a drink was in order with some bread and butter on a plate complimentary.

"I'll tell you what it was for me." And she pulled her spindle-backed chair in under her closer towards the table as it scraped on the hewn wooden floor. "I snapped in my mind up there in Pennsylvania after they had left, Frederick. It was the denigration of the Scottish people and the English speakers of the entire world laughing into our face. And the fact that all of the snotty English leaders in colleges, universities, and schools across the earth were encouraged to make fun of us. Officially and in printed books."

"Honest, Mary, I feel I am lost listening to zees prattle. Vaht are ya talking about?" John kinda of stammered.

"Would you agree if I were to say it is one thing to have a joke made about the country of Scotland?"

"Well sure, English people do that, a lot, but not all of them," Frederick's wife, Mary quipped.

"And for the King to do so?" Mary Patton asked?

"Vell, vie not, he hates everyone!"

"I know," Mary said, "I know. But for them to put that into the world's dictionary for the English language. That's when I snapped, emotionally and spiritually."

"Zertainly," he agreed. "I imagine he hates za Scotch-Irish to zees day for zee Presbyterian Uprising undt (and) zee Battle of the Colonels."[55]

"When a friend told me to look in the new English dictionary of 1755 published by that fat London bastard Samuel Johnson and issued worldwide, under the heading of the letter "O" - I wondered to myself. And then I came to where she had told me, to the word of OATS. And there it was. That's when I saw it on page 1382, the legitimate explanation being taught to children and university students across our globe: **OATS – A grain, which in England generally is given to horses, but in Scotland supports the people.**"

"And people wonder why we hate them!? Mary Dover furthered as she slapped her two hands together with a thunderous clap. Damn them for invading this country again. I swear to it this will be the last damn time that we send their children home in pine boxes!"

"Now, Mary Hambright, don't make a habit of cursing and say you're sorry this instant."

"I'm sorry for denigrating your religious beliefs and kindness. I say I am sorry."

"That was the moment my heart broke, and I shook with anger. My mind snapped, and I went straight home from the book store proudly displaying that two volume set of the new dictionary and I told my John Patton, God bless his soul passed on, that we were leaving and heading down to the wilderness and joining the fight to open up an even larger black powder factory and mill. And my husband started packing right then and there."

"And zen zat is when we heard zixes month later. Zat, you both, had arrived and set you up and started making zee production runs of the various powders to vin vith. And undt, I tell you voman, zat powder you make it is like the lightning rod of the zee almighty. It von zee

---

[55] These are labels you will see in books often printed before the year of 1850. The Presbyterian Uprising means the Revolutionary War wherein the King blamed the damned Presbyterians for stirring up all of the faith groups against England. The Battle of the Colonels is another name used for the Battle of King's Mountain. In maps and books published before the year of 1900, and before the Post Office and mapmakers asked for apostrophes to STOP being used in town names, King's Mountain had an apostrophe in it's name. The local King's Settlement and King family had made quite an impression. Which is where King's Creek also comes from near Hambright Gap – named after Colonel Frederick Hambright.

day for us and drove zem out. And just zo you knows, Mary, vee love oats, oatmeal, porridge, and we make zem vit brown sugar for zee morning vit diced apple in it."

"And I put a handful of raisins and black walnuts in mine Mary so English people in Britain can kiss my, well, kiss my ass! Oops, I cursed again, I'm so sorry Mary. I got overly excited." A Reverend seated across the room heard that and wagged his finger at her.

"You know that one-third of all English forces were removed from this continent the day you won the battle of King's Mountain (she ignored the cursing), don't you Frederick and Mary!? They're smart enough to have figured that out these days, and after changing the textbooks in the schools for our children, we are always called patriots nowadays. No one gets to call me a deviant, say I am promoting terror, or a psychological lunatic anymore.[56] They wrote about us patriots in the papers as outlawed smugglers and called us nothing but bankrupt shopkeepers. They said we had lost our minds to attack the government in America, to meet in secrecy about overthrowing the law and Sherriff. And the final disgrace was that we rebels sent boys home in coffins who were only serving their duty in a foreign land."

"Vell dees time we will drive zem back into the sea to drown and die again vit General Jackson. Dees claims they made ver outrageous. I also know zay gave over 100,000 of zere loyalists free land as rewards across Canada and many of zem have come back undt here, to visit. I even talks vit zem, Mary! We both meets zem and zay family on vacation from zee Canada. Zay have a pension from military service and get zee money. Do I have a pension? Nine. No, I don't."

"Now Fred, don't get upset again about your military service and no pensions. We are doing fine," his wife calmed him. And she stroked his hair and head with her hand and gave him a one-armed hug from chair to chair.

"But every country haz dees pension, except what is our country. Maybe zat change sometime soon."

---

[56] In the 1700's English language you will see this spelled as lunatic.

Mary exclaimed, "And I've got a contract to supply powder to the army to support the war efforts again all the way up to President Madison! You both know that I have always sold my powder direct to the customer and unlike most others, I have avoided middlemen who we caught shorting each pound, stiffing some customers, and even stretching our powder with artificial additives. Since then I have always sold direct. How much did you need this time, Colonel?"

"I have zee money for 48 pounds from you and vee vant a good six pounds just for ourselves," he replied.

"Then let me do it now as I know you are heading out as always."

"Oh no," his wife Mary replied, "we are staying the night and having dinner also. So can we meet in the morning and get it?"

"Oh certainly. I may get up later than usual since we last met. I'm getting older now you know. And I'm going to the fights tonight to bet on my champion I've been supporting financially. Big Roost is ready for another match!"

Now Frederick was wide-eyed and gape-mouthed open. He shakily stood up from the table and steadied himself from his war injury, pointed his right finger at her in accusation and held his left hand over his mouth wheezing in the air as if he had seen a phantom and Zephyr from a graveyard. "You, you, you, YOU!!! You are zee patron of zat monster zat has stolen me clean so many times of mine money!? You are zee financial backer of zat whole team?"

"Now, now Colonel," Mary defended, "You'd better watch your coin bag tonight, or I'll clean you out again!" She laughed so hard, and the Colonel fell forward on the table with his right hand saving himself and grabbing her shoulder with his left hand laughing. Mary Dover Hambright commenced chuckling as she knew all about Fred's darling Silver Tail.

"Oh, mine Got, mine Got, oh mine Got, you are keeling me voman vit you secrets." He sat back down and rocked the chair back a bit when doing so. Each lady could tell he didn't have as much control over his body anymore like he used to as a warfighter.

"You know we may be meeting for the last time, Colonel and Mary," Mary Patton cautioned finally as they all calmed down and she began to butter a slice of Polly's hearth made bread with a provided large, wooden handled knife. "I've been riding these roads for a long time and own over 1500 acres of land at this point and am letting all of my close friends know.

"But zay it is not so, Mary Patton," the Colonel interjected.

"The Sulfur caves for making black powder and bat caves for nitre[57] around my home remain as plentiful as the intense water power needed. The level of premium nitre, charcoal, and sulfur we have been able to conjure up made for a perfect storm to mill black powder. While others across the colonies struggled to find the ingredients, we in the wilderness had it right underfoot. And don't forget my sales techniques of selling direct to the customer increased my take two-fold!"

"We always wondered how you made such excellent, magical black powder at the Patton Mill, and why you moved there to that part of the world," Mary Hambright offered.

Mary finished, "The secret to our charcoal is using some of the finest wood on the planet, and Taylor's explained to me how much pine was right where we live. And let me tell you if you both ever visit my homestead you'll see the secrets to easily find the best nitre, charcoal, and sulfur the world over. But when it comes to the charcoal, well now, making it with that **soft pine is really the truth of what no one has ever known**, Colonel. And mind you, the grandchildren of my own blood don't sound like me when you come, their accents. are brand

---

[57] Part of the hidden and never before revealed secrets of her powder are now, for the first time being cross correlated by this author against Tennessee Forestry Reports, US Geological Surveys, and news reports of the bat population. I cannot find any author who has ever discovered or explained about the perfect storm of all four ingredients: Niter, Charcoal, Sulfer, and Water Power.

new and a blend of many accents. We call it the Southern accent! And in time and history, it's never been heard before. "

"It eez amazing, Mary. Vee are hearing zat new accent grow around here also! I never knew about you pine, you sulfur mines, and secret poopie - and vaz only in zee heat of battle vit your excellent powder. I shot undt killed many men in my time vit it. And as a commander and officer, I alvays felt like I had zee secret veapon on mys side. Zat one zat is unbeatable to kill vit. And it vas all due to you, mine freund, mine friend," Colonel Hambright extended his hand to touch hers and to hold it in his and began to cry with a tear that trickled down his left cheek.

"He's gotten to be like an old softy and wind-bag in his age, Mary," his wife explained.

Mary smiled into his watery eye.

"Vie are you smiling ven I am here crying!?" he blurted.

"Because we get to eat soon and then it's Roost versus Silver!"

Index

#

#MeToo, 1

5

5th NC Regiment, 17

A

A Dictionary of the English Language, 23
A New Voyage to Carolina, 18
Adria Focht, 1
Albert Konetzni, Jr., 1
aliens, 17
Allan B. Miller, 1
Almeda College and University, 1
America, 1, 3, 4, 6, 14, 16, 17, 26, 30, 32, 35, 36, 37, 47
American, iii, iv, 1, 14, 15, 16, 17, 18, 26, 41, 42
American Revolutionary War Living History Center, iii, iv
Andrew Taylor, 37
Anglican, 1, 12
Anglican faith, 1
Antwain Thomas, 1
Appalachia, 3
Art Institute of Charlotte, 1
Art Institute of Pittsburgh, 1
Ashe County, 17
Asheboro, 17
Asheville, 17
Asia, 1
Augusta, 7
Auld Reeky, 32

B

B&B, 25
bannocks, 32
bat caves, 29, 49
bat drippings, 29
Battle of King's Mountain, 46
Battle of the Colonels, 46
Batwoman, 2, 29
Benjamin Cleaveland, 10
Bibby, 10
Biggerstaff's Plantation, 17
Bill Willis, 1
bison, 32
black powder, v, 1, 2, 22, 26, 33, 34, 35, 46, 49
bomb makers, 1
Britain, 17, 47
British, 1, 3, 4, 5, 9, 10, 12, 14, 16, 17, 19, 21, 22, 34, 37
British officer, 4
buffalo, 32
Buncombe County, 17

C

caballos, 17
Camden, 7
Canada, 47
Captain Benjamin Merrill, 5
Captain Carr, 21
Captain Cook's Tavern, 43
Captain James Jack's Tavern, 12
Captain Juan Pardo, 17
Captain Molly, 26
Captain Redhead, 15, 16
Captain Walter Gilkey, 21

Carl White, 1
Carlisle, 14, 26, 30, 31, 36
Carole Plonk Haas Gravagno, 1
Carter, 26
castle, 6, 24
Catawba, 11, 15, 34, 35
Cecil D. Haney, 1
charcoal, 28, 29, 49
Charles Town, SC, 18
Charlestown, 11, 42
Charlotte, v, 1, 11, 18, 41, 43
Charlottesburg, 1, 11
Charlottesburgh, 1
Charlottetown, 1, 11, 12, 14, 34
Cherokee, 16, 34
China, 23
Christ, 24
churning butter, 23
City Colleges of Chicago, 1
civil war, 1
Civil War, 26
Claire Fraser, 29
clapshot, 32
Cleveland, iv, 10
Cock a Leeky, 32
cock-a-leekie soup, 32
colcannon, 32
Colonel, 3, 4, 5, 7, 8, 9, 10, 17, 19, 22, 25, 36, 42, 43, 46, 48, 49, 50
Colonel Ambrose Mills, 5
Colonel Cleaveland, 9, 22
Colonel Edward Buncombe, 17
Colonel Hambright, 9, 50
Colonel Hampton, 7, 8
Colonel John Sevier, 4, 25, 36
Colonel Mills, 8, 10
Colonel Sevier, 3, 4, 25
Colonel Shelby, 7
Colonel Tarleton, 19
Conestoga, 12
Conestoga Valley, 14
Conestoga wagon, 12
Confederacy, 26
Continental Congress, 17, 29

Cornwallis, v
Corolla, 17
cottage pie, 32
Craig Schreiber, 1
crowns, 14
Culloden, 4

D

David Jones, 1
David Sherrill, 1
David Unnasch, 1
Dean, and Anne Ornish, 1
Deneise Deter Liss, 1
deviants, 1
Doctor, 1, 3, 4
Dollywood, 3
Dr. Uzal Johnson, 3
Dragoons, 5, 15
drawn and quartered, 5
Duke of Cumberland, 4

E

earth, 1, 7, 10, 23, 33, 40, 41, 45
Edinburgh, 32
Edith Morgan, 1
Elizabeth Wilson Taylor, 37
England, 26, 33, 42, 46
English, 1, 17, 21, 23, 45, 46, 47
Europe, 1, 14, 32

F

Federal Reserve, 14
flax, 22, 30
forbidden zone, 23
Forestry Reports, 49
Fort San Juan, 17
France, 32
Frank Panzone, 1
Frederick Hambright, 42, 46
Free Republic of Franklin, 31

Freedom Bell, 18
French revolution, 42

G

Gatlinburg, 3
General, v, 18, 33, 37, 47
George the III, 5
Germantown, 17
Gilkey, 10
glass ceilings, v
gold, 3, 14, 16
Governor, 4, 5, 6, 7, 12, 17, 25, 36
Governor Tryon, 7, 12
Green Corn Ceremony, 35
Grover, NC, iv
guano, 29, 33
guinea, 14
Gunther, 5, 6, 7, 9, 10

H

Hambright Gap, 46
Hampton, 10
hangings, 5, 8
Hank Weddington, 1
Hawaii, 1
Hernando de Soto, 17
Hessian, 5
Hez Alexander, 12
Hezekiah Alexander, 12, 14, 18
his Majesty, 5
Hobbs, 10
hornet's nest, 20
Howard Burnham, 1
Hyder, 26

I

Indian Nation, 15
Indians, 15, 18, 34, 36, 37
innkeeper, 25
Irish, 3, 14, 26, 32, 33, 42, 46

Ishmael Titus, 18, 19
Italians, 32

J

James McKee, 3
James Thomas, v
Jamestown, VA, 17
Jason Falls, 1
Jeff Trexler, 16, 19, 27, 44
John Lawson, 17, 18
John Patton, 23, 24, 25, 26, 46
John Wayne, 3
John Wheeley **Lea**, 33
Johnson, 4, 5, 23, 46
Jonesborough, 28, 31
Joseph J. Krol, 1

K

kaya, 35
Ken Unnasch, 1
Kentucky, 3
Kerri (Tuttle) Johann, 2
Kim Hambright, 1
King family, 46
King George, 12, 35
King Hagler, 15
King Hobbs, 46
King's Creek, 46
King's Mountain, v, 3, 5, 17, 22, 42, 46, 47
King's Settlement, 46
Kings Mountain, v, 36
Kitchen Bouquet, 32
Kitty Hawk, 17

L

Lancaster, 11
Lance Bacchia, 1
Laura Hope-Gill, 1
Legion, 19
Lenoir Rhyne University, 1
Leslie McKesson, 1

Lesser Franklin, 31
Limestone Springs, 42
linen, 6, 21, 30
Lisa Fournier, 1
lobster, 6, 19, 21
London, 18, 23, 46
Long House headquarters, 15
long rifle, 20, 21
Luciano Bacchia, 1

M

Madison, 48
Major Ferguson, 3
Major Patrick Ferguson, 5
Major William Chronicle, 3
Marc Pelaez, 1
Margaret, 28
Mark Anthony, 1
Martin Academy, 28
Martin CJ Mongiello, iv
Mary Dover, 42, 46, 48
Mary Dover Hambright, 42, 48
Mary Ellen Sloan Hinson, 18
Mary Ludwig Hays McCauly, 26
Mary McKeehan, 26
Mary Patton, v, 2, 22, 23, 45, 49
Mary Sample Alexander, 14
Master of the Royal Mint, 14
Mayflower, 17
McFall, 10
Mecklenburg County, 18
Michael Gaffney, 42
Mill's, 6
Mills, 6, 10
Mississippi River, 26
Molly Pitcher, 26
Monmouth, NJ, 26
Morganton, 17
Morristown, 17
Murtagh Fraser, 4
Museum, v, 18
Mustang horses, 17

N

National Park Service, 1
Navy, 12
NC, v, 1, 5, 17, 18
New Jersey, 4, 34
New York, 5, 7, 30, 44
Ninety-Six, 7
Nitre, 29
Norma Lee Hackney, 2
North Carolina, 4, 5, 7, 15, 17, 18, 26, 31

O

OATS, 46
Operation Enduring Freedom, 2
Operation Iraqi Freedom, 2
Orion, 7
Orlando Herrera, 1
Outlander, 29
outlaws, 1

P

P's and Q's, 16
palace, 6, 24
paper cartridges, 21
Paris, 44
Patrick J. Casey, 1
Patrick W. Mullen III, 2
patriots, 7, 47
Pennsylvania, 11, 12, 14, 20, 25, 26, 34, 35, 45
Philadelphia, 11, 17, 29, 30, 34
Plymouth, 17
Polly, 42, 43, 44, 45, 49
Portuguese, 14
potassium nitrate, 28, 29
Pound Scots coins, 14
pound sterling, 14
Presbyterian, 12, 46
Presbyterians, 46
President, 18, 37, 48
Prince Harry, 1
Prince William, 4

Princess Meghan, 1
prison, 1
prisoners, 1, 3, 5, 17
Private Titus, 20
Prussian, 43
psychological lunatic, 47
psychos, 1

Q

Queen Elizabeth, 1
Queen's College, 12

R

Rania, v
rebels, 1, 5, 21, 22, 47
red ants, 20
Reg Alexander, 1
Regulators, 5
Republic of Watauga, 31
Reverend Samuel Doak, 28
Revolutionary War, iii, iv, 26, 46
Richard Smith, 1
Rick Moore, 1
Robert Morris, 17
Robin Hood, 6
Rock Hill, 15

S

Sally New River, 15, 35
saltpeter, 26, 28, 29
Sam Adams, 12
Samuel Ashe, 17
Samuel Johnson, 46
scones, 23, 32
Scot-Irish, 3
Scotland, 4, 32, 45, 46
Scott Syfert, 1
Scottish, 3, 32, 45
Senator, 17, 37
Sevier, 4, 25, 26, 36

Shankless Buckeye, 12
shepherds pie, 32
Sheriff, 5
Sheriff of Nottingham, 6
shillings, 14
shortbread, 32
silver, 14, 21, 40
Sir Isaac Newton, 14
Society, Colonial Dames, 18
soda bread, 32
South Carolina, 3, 15, 16, 18, 34, 42
Southern accent, 50
Southwest Territory, 31
Spaetzle, 43
Spanish, 14, 17
St. Christopher, 17
St. Kitts, 17
State of Frankland, 31
State of Franklin, 26, 31
states paper money, 14
Stinking Billy flowers, 4
Stormy, v, 2
Submarine Warfare pin, 2
sulfur, 28, 29, 33, 49, 50
Surface Warfare pin, 2
Surveyor General Of North Carolina, 18
sweet potato, 5
Sweet William, 4
Sycamore Shoals, v

T

Tampa, FL, 17
Taylor, 26, 30, 31, 35, 36, 37, 45, 49
teachers, 1
Tennessee, 26, 31, 33, 36, 49
terror, 21, 41, 47
Terrorist, 1
Thanksgiving, 39
The Lost Colony, 17
Thickety Creek, 43
Thomas Toglia, 1
Thomas Turner, 1
Thomas Wolfe Institute, 1

Tim Moore, 1
TimesUp, v, 1
Titanic, 32
tomato, 32
Tories, 34
Travis McVey, 1
trifle, 32
Troy State University, 1
Tryon, 5, 6, 7, 12
Tryon County, 7
Tryon Mountain, 7
Tryon Palace, 5, 7
Tryon Park, 7
Tryon School, 7

U

United Colonies, 16, 31
United Kingdom, 4
United States, 16, 17, 26
upcountry, 3, 42
Uprising, 46
US Geological Survey, 33
USS Anzio, 2
USS Dwight D. Eisenhower, 2
USS Saipan, 2

V

Valentine, 36
Virginia, 25

W

War of Independence, 42
Washington, 18, 31, 33, 37
Washington County, 31
Watauga Association, 31, 36
Will Upchurch, 1
William Hays, 26
William Henry **Perrins**, 33
William Richard King, 1
Wilmington, 4, 11, 17
women, v, 1, 10, 11, 13, 15, 21, 34, 35, 43
Women in War, 2
Wonder Woman, 2
Wondra, 32
Worcester, 33
Worcestershire, 33

Bibliography

Adams, E. C. (2014). *A Prelude to Revolution: Scots-Irish Vigilantes in the Colonial Backcountry*. Retrieved from

Alderman, P. (1990). *One Heroic Hour at King's Mountain*: The Overmountain Press.

Alexander, D., & Alexander, J. (2009). *The History of Mecklenburg County [Nc]*: Genealogical Publishing Com.

Allen, D. (2018). *Irish traditional cooking*: Kyle Books.

Arthur, J. P. (1992). *A History of Watauga County, North Carolina*: The Overmountain Press.

Ballard, B. (2019). The Song of the Churn.

Barden, L. S. (1997). Historic prairies in the Piedmont of North and South Carolina, USA. *Natural Areas Journal*, 149-152.

Beck Jr, R. A. (1997). From Joara to Chiaha: Spanish Exploration of the Appalachian Summit Area, 1540-1568. *Southeastern Archaeology*, 162-169.

Beck Jr, R. A., Moore, D. G., & Rodning, C. B. (2006). Identifying Fort San Juan: A Sixteenth-Century Spanish Occupation at the Berry Site, North Carolina. *Southeastern Archaeology*, 65-77.

Beck, R. A., Fritz, G. J., Lapham, H. A., Moore, D. G., & Rodning, C. B. (2016). The Politics of Provisioning: Food and Gender at Fort San Juan De Joara, 1566–1568. *American Antiquity, 81*(1), 3-26.

Bell, A. (1893). SANITARY ADVANTAGES OF SOUTH CAROLINA--HER PINE FORESTS AND MINERAL SPRINGS. *The Sanitarian (1873-1904), 30*(282), 415.

Bennett, M. "A Song for Every Cow She Milked..." Sharing the Work and Sharing the Voices among the Gaels.

Bentley, M. M. (1991). The Slaveholding Catawbas. *The South Carolina Historical Magazine, 92*(2), 85-98.

Berkin, C. (2007). *Revolutionary Mothers: Women in the Struggle for America's Independence*: Vintage.

Boswell, J. (1873). *The Life of Samuel Johnson*: William P. Nimmo.

Braun, E. M. (2019). *The Real George Washington: The Truth Behind the Legend*: Compass Point Books.

Brewster, D. (2010). *Memoirs of the life, writings, and discoveries of Sir Isaac Newton* (Vol. 2): Cambridge University Press.

Broadwater, J., & Kickler, T. L. (2019). *North Carolina's Revolutionary Founders*: UNC Press Books.

Brown Jr, R. W. (2009). *Kings Mountain and Cowpens: Our Victory Was Complete*: Arcadia Publishing.

Brown, P. H. (1908). *A short history of Scotland*: Oliver and Boyd.

Brudvig, L. A., Grman, E., Habeck, C. W., Orrock, J. L., & Ledvina, J. A. (2013). Strong legacy of agricultural land use on soils and understory plant communities in longleaf pine woodlands. *Forest Ecology and Management, 310*, 944-955.

Byerley, J. S. (2018). Mentoring in the Era of# MeToo. *Jama, 319*(12), 1199-1200.

Caldwell, J. W. (1898). THE WAUTAUGA ASSOCIATION. *Tennessee Historical Quarterly, 3*(4), 312.

Chaplin, J. E. (2012). *An Anxious Pursuit: agricultural innovation and modernity in the Lower South, 1730-1815*: UNC Press Books.

Chojnacky, D. C., & Schuler, T. M. (2004). Amounts of down woody materials for mixed-oak forests in Kentucky, Virginia, Tennessee, and North Carolina. *Southern Journal of Applied Forestry, 28*(2), 113-117.

Conkin, P. (1955). The Church Establishment in North Carolina, 1765-1776. *The North Carolina Historical Review, 32*(1), 1-30.

Cox, W. E., & Cox, J. (2011). *An American Saga: Some East Tennessee Taylors*: iUniverse.

Craig, J. (1963). Isaac Newton and the counterfeiters. *Notes and Records of the Royal Society of London, 18*(2), 136-145.

Cranford, D. J. (2018). *Catawba Household Variation in the Late Eighteenth Century.* The University of North Carolina at Chapel Hill,

Crawford, E. W. (1999). *Samuel Doak: Pioneer Missionary in East Tennessee*: The Overmountain Press.

Crow, J. J. (1978). Tory Plots and Anglican Loyalty: The Llewelyn Conspiracy of 1777. *The North Carolina Historical Review, 55*(1), 1-17.

Davis Jr, R. S., & Riggs, B. H. (2006). A SUMMARY REPORT OF 2005 ARCHAEOLOGICAL INVESTIGATIONS AT CATAWBA NEW TOWN, LANCASTER COUNTY, SOUTH CAROLINA.

Davis, S., & Riggs, B. (2004). An Introduction to the Catawba Project. *North Carolina Archaeology, 53*, 1-41.

De Vorsey, L. (1978). Amerindian contributions to the mapping of North America: A preliminary view. *Imago Mundi, 30*(1), 71-78.

DeMond, R. O. (1979). *The Loyalists in North Carolina During the Revolution*: Genealogical Publishing Com.

DePratter, C. B., Hudson, C. M., & Smith, M. T. (1983). The route of Juan Pardo's explorations in the interior Southeast, 1566-1568. *The Florida Historical Quarterly, 62*(2), 125-158.

DePratter, C. B., & Smith, M. T. (1987). Sixteenth century European trade in the southeastern United States: evidence from the Juan Pardo expeditions (1566-1568). *Notebook, 19*(1-4), 52.

DeSantis, L. R., & Wallace, S. C. (2008). Neogene forests from the Appalachians of Tennessee, USA: geochemical evidence from fossil mammal teeth. *Palaeogeography, Palaeoclimatology, Palaeoecology, 266*(1-2), 59-68.

Devine, T. M. (1995). *Exploring the Scottish past: themes in the history of Scottish society*: Dundurn.

Dixon, M. (1989). *The Wataugans*: The Overmountain Press.

Dunkerly, R. (2007). *Women of the Revolution: Bravery and Sacrifice on the Southern Battlefields*: Arcadia Publishing.

Dunkerly, R. M. (2007). *The Battle of Kings Mountain: Eyewitness Accounts*: Arcadia Publishing.

Dykeman, W. (1978). *The battle of Kings Mountain, 1780, with fire and sword*: Government Printing Office.

Ewen, C., Samford, P. M., & Mathewes, P. (2002). The Sauthier Maps and the Formal Gardens at Tryon Palace: Myth or Reality? *The North Carolina Historical Review, 79*(3), 327-346.

FitzGibbon, T. (1983). *Irish traditional food*: St. Martin's Press.

Foster, I. (1971). Washington College and Washington College Academy. *Tennessee Historical Quarterly, 30*(3), 241.

Freeze, G. (1979). Like A House Built Upon Sand: The Anglican Church and Establishment in North Carolina, 1765-1776. *Historical Magazine of the Protestant Episcopal Church, 48*(4), 405-432.

Frost, C. (2007). History and future of the longleaf pine ecosystem. In *The longleaf pine ecosystem* (pp. 9-48): Springer.

Gannon, M. V. (1965). Sebastián Montero, pioneer American missionary, 1566-1572. *The Catholic Historical Review, 51*(3), 335-353.

Gentilcore, D. (2010). *Pomodoro!: a history of the tomato in Italy*: Columbia University Press.

Gibson, A., & Smout, T. (1989). SCOTTISH FOOD AND SCOTTISH. *Scottish society, 1500-1800*, 59.

Gilbert, E., & Gilbert, C. (2015). *Patriot Militiaman in the American Revolution 1775–82*: Bloomsbury Publishing.

Gilbert, E., & Gilbert, C. (2016). *Cowpens 1781: Turning Point of the American Revolution*: Bloomsbury Publishing.

Graham, N. (2008). North Carolina Books compiled by. *North Carolina Libraries, 64*(3), 76-80.

Gustafson, T. (1992). *Representative words: politics, literature, and the American language, 1776-1865* (Vol. 60): Cambridge University Press.

Hall, A. R. (1948). 1. Sir Isaac Newton's Note-Book, 1661–65. *Cambridge historical journal, 9*(2), 239-250.

Hamilton, D. J. (2016). Scotland in the eighteenth century. In *Scotland, the Caribbean and the Atlantic world 1750–1820*: Manchester University Press.

Hartgrove, W. (1916). The Negro Soldier in the American Revolution. *The Journal of Negro History, 1*(2), 110-131.

Haywood, M. D. L. (1903). *Governor William Tryon, And His Administration in the Province of North Carolina, 1765-1771: Services in a Civil Capacity and Military Career as Commander-in-chief of Colonial Forces which Suppressed the Insurrection of the Regulators*: EM Uzzell, printer.

Henson, S. L. A. (2005). To See Her Face, To Hear Her Voice: Profiling the Place of Women in Early Upper East Tennessee, 1773-1810.

Hetherington, N. S. (1983). Isaac Newton's influence on Adam Smith's natural laws in economics. *Journal of the History of Ideas, 44*(3), 497-505.

Holroyd-Leduc, J. M., & Straus, S. E. (2018). # MeToo and the medical profession. In: Can Med Assoc.

Horton, J. (1984). Stratigraphic nomenclature in the Kings Mountain belt, North Carolina and South Carolina.

Houston, R. A., & Whyte, I. D. (2005). *Scottish Society, 1500-1800*: Cambridge University Press.

Howard, R. A. (1975). Black Powder Manufacture. *IA. The Journal of the Society for Industrial Archeology*, 13-28.

Hudson, A. P. (1947). Songs of the North Carolina Regulators. *The William and Mary Quarterly: A Magazine of Early American History and Culture*, 470-485.

Hunter, C. L. (1877). *Sketches of Western North Carolina, Historical and Biographical: Illustrating Principally the Revolutionary Period of Mecklenburg, Rowan, Lincoln, and Adjoining Counties, Accompanied with Miscellaneous Information, Much of it Never Before Published*: Raleigh News Steam Job Print.

Jagsi, R. (2018). Sexual harassment in medicine—# MeToo. *New England Journal of Medicine, 378*(3), 209-211.

Johnson, S. (1828). *Johnson's Dictionary Improved by Todd: Abridged... with the Addition of Walker's Pronunciation*: B. Perkins & Company.

Johnson, S. (1877). *A Dictionary of the English Language: In which the Words are Deduced from Their Originals; and Illustrated in Their Different Significations by Examples from the Best Writers. To which are Prefixed, a History of the Language, and an English Grammar*: Reeves and Turner.

Johnston, C., & Spencer, C. (1905). *Ireland's Story: A Short History of Ireland for Schools, Reading Circles, and General Readers*: Houghton, Mifflin.

Kars, M. (2002). *Breaking Loose Together: The Regulator Rebellion in Pre-Revolutionary North Carolina*: Univ of North Carolina Press.

Kay, M. L. M. (1965). Provincial Taxes in North Carolina during the Administrations of Dobbs and Tryon. *The North Carolina Historical Review, 42*(4), 440-453.

Kearl, H. (2018). The Facts Behind the# metoo Movement: A National Study on Sexual Harassment and Assault (Executive Summary).

King, M. E. (2019). Communication and Collective Mentality: Pathways of Mobilisation in Colonial America. *Brief Encounters, 3*(1).

Kliebhan, B., & Thomas, N. (2008). *Searching for Max.* Paper presented at the Max Kämper centennial symposium and 9th science symposium, Mammoth Cave National Park.

Kopel, D. B. (2011). How the British Gun Control Program Precipitated the American Revolution. *Charleston L. Rev., 6*, 283.

Kornblum, L. S. (1984). Women Warriors in a Men's World: The Combat Exclusion. *Law & Ineq., 2*, 351.

Kramer, L. J. (1953). MUSKETS IN THE PULPIT: 1776—1783. *Journal of the Presbyterian Historical Society (1943-1961)*, 229-244.

Landis, J. B. (1905). *A Short History of Molly Pitcher, the Heroine of the Battle of Monmouth*: Cornman Print. Company for the District of Cumberland County POS of A. of ….

Lawson, J. (1709). A new voyage to Carolina: containing the exact description and natural history of that country; together with the present state thereof; and a journal of a thousand miles, travel'd thro' several nations of Indians; giving a particular account of their customs, manners, etc.

Lee, M. (2019). *Our Lost Declaration: America's Fight Against Tyranny from King George to the Deep State*: Sentinel.

Lewis, J. A. (1980). The Royal Gunpowder Monopoly in New Spain (1766-1783): A Case Study of Management, Technology, and Reform Under Charles III. *Ibero-amerikanisches Archiv, 6*(4), 355-372.

Lin, T., Zhu, G., Zhang, J., Xu, X., Yu, Q., Zheng, Z., . . . Wang, X. (2014). Genomic analyses provide insights into the history of tomato breeding. *Nature genetics, 46*(11), 1220.

Lindgren, W. (1972). Agricultural Propaganda in Lawson's" A New Voyage to Carolina". *The North Carolina Historical Review, 49*(4), 333-344.

Mac Con Iomaire, M., & Cashman, D. (2011). Irish culinary manuscripts and printed books: a discussion.

Mack, W. P., & Konetzni, A. H. (1982). *Command at sea*: US Naval Institute Press.

MacKay, A. (1891). THE SONGS AND BALLADS OF FIFE. *Blackwood's Edinburgh magazine, 150*(911), 334-347.

Malone, M. T. (1970). Sketches of the Anglican Clergy Who Served in North Carolina During the Period, 1765-1776. *Historical Magazine of the Protestant Episcopal Church, 39*(2), 137-161.

Mason, L. (2004). *Food Culture in Great Britain*: Greenwood Publishing Group.

McConville, B. (2012). *The King's Three Faces: The Rise and Fall of Royal America, 1688-1776*: UNC Press Books.

McGill, J. (1925). Franklin and Frankland: Names and Boundaries. *Tennessee Historical Magazine, 8*(4), 248-257.

McLachlan, S. (2011). *Medieval Handgonnes: The first black powder infantry weapons*: Bloomsbury Publishing.

Mendes, K., Ringrose, J., & Keller, J. (2018). # MeToo and the promise and pitfalls of challenging rape culture through digital feminist activism. *European Journal of Women's Studies, 25*(2), 236-246.

Merrell, J. H. (1984). The Indians' New World: The Catawba Experience. *The William and Mary Quarterly: A Magazine of Early American History and Culture*, 538-565.

Mitchell, H. L. (2004). Springs of South Carolina. *South Carolina State Documents Depository*.

Moore, D. G., Beck Jr, R. A., & Rodning, C. B. (2004). Joara and Fort San Juan: culture contact at the edge of the world. *Antiquity, 78*(299), 1566-1568.

Multhauf, R. P. (1971). The French Crash Program for Saltpeter Production, 1776-94. *Technology and Culture, 12*(2), 163-181.

Munroe, C. E. (1896). ON THE DEVELOPMENT OF SMOKELESS POWDER. *Journal of the American Chemical Society, 18*(9), 819-846.

Nelson, J. K. (2003). *A blessed company: Parishes, parsons, and parishioners in Anglican Virginia, 1690-1776*: Univ of North Carolina Press.

Nelson, P. D. (1990). *William Tryon and the Course of Empire: A Life in British Imperial Service*: UNC Press Books.

Nugent, J., & Clark, M. (2010). A loaded plate: food symbolism and the early modern Scottish household. *Journal of Scottish Historical Studies, 30*(1), 43-63.

Oates, J. D. (2015). *The Jacobite campaigns: the British state at war*: Routledge.

O'Dell, G. A. (1989). Bluegrass Powdermen: A Sketch of the Industry. *The Register of the Kentucky Historical Society, 87*(2), 99-117.

O'Donnell III, J. H. (1991). The Indians' New World: Catawbas and Their Neighbors from European Contact through the Era of Removal. In: JSTOR.

Oliver, J. (2011). *Jamie's Great Britain*: Penguin.

O'Steen, N. (1976). Pioneer Education in the Tennessee Country. *Tennessee Historical Quarterly, 35*(2), 199-219.

Paine, T. (1776). *Common Sense: 1776*: Infomotions, Incorporated.

Peralta, I. E., Spooner, D. M., Razdan, M., & Mattoo, A. (2006). History, origin and early cultivation of tomato (Solanaceae). *Genetic improvement of solanaceous crops, 2*, 1-27.

PettyJohn, M. E., Muzzey, F. K., Maas, M. K., & McCauley, H. L. (2018). # HowIWillChange: Engaging men and boys in the# MeToo movement. *Psychology of Men & Masculinity*.

Plumer, R. P. (2014). *Charlotte and the American Revolution: Reverend Alexander Craighead, the Mecklenburg Declaration and the Foothills Fight for Independence*: Arcadia Publishing.

Powell, W. S. (1989). *North Carolina through four centuries*: Univ of North Carolina Press.

Powell, W. S., & Hill, M. (2010). *The North Carolina gazetteer: a dictionary of Tar Heel places and their history*: Univ of North Carolina Press.

Quinn, D. (2017). *The Roanoke Voyages, 1584-1590: Documents to illustrate the English Voyages to North America under the Patent granted to Walter Raleigh in 1584 Volumes I-II*: Routledge.

Ramsey, J. G. M. (1853). *The Annals of Tennessee to the End of the Eighteenth Century: Comprising Its Settlement, as the Watauga Association, from 1769 to 1777*: J. Russell.

Rankin, H. F. (2005). *The North Carolina Continentals*: UNC Press Books.

Ready, M. (2005). *The Tar Heel State: A History of North Carolina*: Univ of South Carolina Press.

Region, S. (2005). Southern Campaigns of the Revolutionary War Phase III: Research in the United States.

Royster, C. (2011). *A Revolutionary People at War: The Continental Army and American Character, 1775-1783*: The University of North Carolina Press.

Salav, D. L. (1975). The Production of Gunpowder in Pennsylvania during the American Revolution. *The Pennsylvania Magazine of History and Biography, 99*(4), 422-442.

Salley, A. S. (1907). The Mecklenburg Declaration: The Present Status of the Question. *The American Historical Review, 13*(1), 16-43.

Sasse, R. A. (1981). *The influence of physical properties on black powder combustion*. Retrieved from

Schafer, D. L. (1992). The Papers of Henry Laurens, Volume Eleven: January 5, 1776-November 1, 1777. In: JSTOR.

Schaw, J. (2005). *Journal of a Lady of Quality: Being the Narrative of a Journey from Scotland to the West Indies, North Carolina, and Portugal, in the Years 1774-1776*: U of Nebraska Press.

Schlesinger, A. M. (1918). *The colonial merchants and the American Revolution, 1763-1776*: Columbia University.

Schweikart, L., & Dougherty, D. (2017). *The Politically Incorrect Guide to the American Revolution*: Simon and Schuster.

Sepich, J. E. (1993). A" bloody dark pastryman": Cormac McCarthy's Recipe for Gunpowder and Historical Fiction in" Blood Meridian". *The Mississippi Quarterly, 46*(4), 547-563.

Sexton, R. (1998). *A little history of Irish food*: Dublin Institute of Technology.

Shain, B. A. (2016). The First American Declaration of Independence? The Disputed History of the Mecklenburg Declaration of May 20, 1775 by Scott Syfert. *Register of the Kentucky Historical Society, 114*(3), 486-489.

Shanahan, M. (2015). 'Whipt with a twig rod': Irish manuscript recipe books as sources for the study of culinary material culture, c. 1660 to 1830. *Proceedings of the Royal Irish Academy. Section C: Archaeology, Celtic Studies, History, Linguistics, Literature, 115*, 197-218.

Shebalin, T. M. (2011). *Domestic Activities and Household Variation at Catawba New Town ca. 1790–1820.* The University of North Carolina at Chapel Hill,

Shirras, G. F., & Craig, J. (1945). Sir Isaac Newton and the currency. *The Economic Journal, 55*(218/219), 217-241.

Shoemaker, N. (2006). *A strange likeness: Becoming red and white in eighteenth-century North America*: Oxford University Press.

Smith, A. F. (2001). *The tomato in America: early history, culture, and cookery*: University of Illinois Press.

Smout, T. C. (2005). *Anglo-scottish relations from 1603 to 1900* (Vol. 127): Oxford University Press.

Sohn, M. (2005). *Appalachian Home Cooking: History, Culture, and Recipes*: University Press of Kentucky.

Spindel, D. J. (1980). Law and Disorder: The North Carolina Stamp Act Crisis. *The North Carolina Historical Review, 57*(1), 1-16.

Stephenson, O. W. (1925). The Supply of Gunpowder in 1776. *The American Historical Review, 30*(2), 271-281.

Stumpf, V. O. (1986). *Josiah Martin: The Last Royal Governor of North Carolina*: Carolina Academic Press for the Kellenberger Historical Foundation.

Swan Jr, P. G. (2013). Grace Ellen McCrann Memorial Lecture:"The Present Defenceless State of the Country": Gunpowder Plots in Revolutionary South Carolina.

Syfert, S. (2013). *The First American Declaration of Independence?: The Disputed History of the Mecklenburg Declaration of May 20, 1775*: McFarland.

Syfert, S. (2018). *Eminent Charlotteans: Twelve Historical Profiles from North Carolina's Queen City*: McFarland.

Thorp, D. B. (1996). Taverns and tavern culture on the Southern colonial frontier: Rowan County, North Carolina, 1753-1776. *The Journal of Southern History, 62*(4), 661-688.

Tippett, E. C. (2018). The Legal Implications of the MeToo Movement. *Minn. L. Rev., 103*, 229.

Tompkins, D. A. (1903). *History of Mecklenburg County and the City of Charlotte, from 1740 to 1903*: Higginson Book Company.

Vissage, J. S., & Duncan, K. (1990). Forest statistics for Tennessee counties-1989. *Resour. Bull. SO-148. New Orleans, Louisiana: US Department of Agriculture, Forest Service, Southern Forest Experiment Station. 72 p., 148*.

Walker, M. A. (2013). *The Battles of Kings Mountain and Cowpens: The American Revolution in the Southern Backcountry*: Routledge.

Watson, A. D. (1979). The Anglican Parish In Royal North Carolina, 1729-1775. *Historical Magazine of the Protestant Episcopal Church, 48*(3), 303-319.

Wear, D. N., & Greis, J. G. (2002). Southern Forest Resource Assessment-Summary Report. *Gen. Tech. Rep. SRS-54. Asheville, NC: US Department of Agriculture, Forest Service, Southern Research Station. 103 p., 54.*

Weightman, G. (2010). *The Industrial Revolutionaries: The Making of the Modern World, 1776–1914*: Open Road+ Grove/Atlantic.

Weller, J. (1962). Revolutionary War Artillery in the South. *The Georgia Historical Quarterly, 46*(3), 250-273.

Wilson, J. K. (1990). Religion under the state constitutions, 1776-1800. *Journal of Church and State*, 753-773.

Wofford, B. E., & Chester, E. W. (2002). *Guide to the trees, shrubs, and woody vines of Tennessee*: Univ. of Tennessee Press.

Wolfe, M. R. (1996). The Feminine Dimension in the Volunteer State. *Tennessee Historical Quarterly, 55*(2), 112.

Zarkov, D., & Davis, K. (2018). Ambiguities and dilemmas around# Metoo:# forhow long and# whereto? In: Sage Publications Sage UK: London, England.

Ziemke, P. C. (1952). Early methods of saltpeter production. *Journal of Chemical Education, 29*(9), 466.

Zimmerman, E. I. (1996). *Bristol to Knoxville: A Postcard Tour*: Arcadia Publishing.